Theatre Lighting: An Illustrated Glossary

by
Albert F. C. Wehlburg

Drama Book Specialists (Publishers)
New York

All rights reserved under the International and Pan American Copyright
Conventions. For information address Drama Book Specialists (Publishers),
150 West 52nd Street, New York, New York 10019.

Library of Congress Cataloging in Publication Data

Wehlburg, Albert F C
    Theatre lighting.

    1. Stage lighting—Terminology. I. Title.
PN2091.E4W4   792′.025   75-19332
ISBN 0-910482-69-1

Printed in the United States of America

AUTHOR'S NOTE

Theatre stage lighting is one of the most rapidly growing and developing segments of modern theatre. Several factors have contributed to this growth. There has been an upsurge of interest in modern theatre. The development of sophisticated sound equipment for theatre has forced lighting designers to produce more complex lighting designs and effects to relate to the new sounds. A tremendous factor has been the development of new dimming systems. The electronic light boards and the even more radical memory boards are freeing the lighting designer to think in totally new areas. The performance capabilities of these new lighting devices have never before been possible.

Because of the new influx of equipment it has become necessary that a standard vocabulary be developed so that the lighting technicians and the lighting designers from all parts of the country may communicate in the same language.

Through my contacts with professional theatres, touring theatres, community theatres, collegiate theatres, and through reading numerous texts I have developed a vocabulary list which favors the most often used terms with definitions as they are generally used. I am aware that in each theatre there will be terms which are peculiar to that theatre and such terms have not been included in this vocabulary. The intent was to select and to identify those terms which are in general use around the country.

Albert Wehlburg I.A.T.S.E. Local 360
Technical Director/Lighting Designer, University of Florida
Gainesville, Florida
1975

ABERRATIONS Any disturbance of the rays of a beam of light so that it can no longer be brought to a sharp focus or form a clear image.

ABSORPTION FILTER A plastic or gelatine material (often called a "gel") which permits certain light waves to pass through while absorbing other colors.

ACCESS TIME The time it takes for a memory system on a light board to be able to accept information and to make it available to the operator.

ACCURACY A reference to the setting of a potentiometer and the actual output voltage of a dimmer. It is usually given in per cent.

AC/DC Said of electronic equipment which may be operated on either ac or dc current as the primary power source.

ACETATE A plastic-like material made from one of the salts of acetic acid. It is normally sold in sheets and may be painted with designs for use with Linnebach projectors.

AC GENERATOR (See Generator)

ACHROMATIC Said of a lens which transmits light without separating it into its spectral colors. Spotlight lenses should be achromatic.

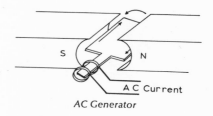
AC Generator

AC POWER SUPPLY A source which provides ac power; often used in terms of a variable voltage tap transformer.

ACTING AREA That area of the stage used by the performers when they are seen by the audience.

ACTIVE CURRENT A term used to describe an electrical circuit which has some type of instrument on it in actual use.

ADAPTOR A short length of wire with connectors; used between a receptacle and equipment having different types of plugs. (See Socket Adaptor)

ADDITIVE COLOR The mixing of two colors of light; e.g., to create the secondary colors in light we use the additive system of two primary colors. The painted surface does not "color" the beam of light; it merely reflects the color it is capable of reflecting. Adding primaries of light leads to white light.

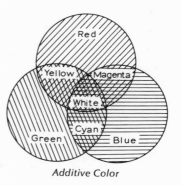
Additive Color

ADJUSTABLE WRENCH An open end wrench which may be adjusted to the size of the bolt it may function on. Adjustable wrenches are often used to connect "C" clamps to battens and to tighten light instruments so that they will not change focus.

Adjustable Wrench

ADMITTANCE The measure of ease with which an alternating current may flow through a circuit.

AERIAL CABLE A cable which is strung overhead.

AFTER GLOW The light which remains in a gas discharge tube after the power has been shut off.

AIR GAP The open, non-conductive space between electrical contacts. (See Contact Gap)

ALBEDO The reflective ability of a surface when compared to the amount of light it receives.

Alligator Clip

ALLIGATOR CLIP A small, spring-loaded, metal clip often used to temporarily jump a circuit for testing purposes.

ALIGNMENT PIN Any type of pin or fin which insures the proper positioning of a potentiometer or pre-amp in an autotransformer dimmer.

ALIVE Said of an electrical circuit which carries a charge different from that of the ground or earth system.

ALKALINE CELL An alkaline-manganese, primary cell which has about 100% more capacity for containing current than the zinc-carbon cell.

ALLEN SCREW A machine screw with a hexagonal socket in its head. Often found in the lamp alignment mechanism of an ellipsoidal reflector.

ALTERNATING CURRENT (AC) Current that reverses direction 120 times, or makes 60 complete cycles, per second. Transformers, autotransformers, and electronic boards require ac current.

ALTERNATING VOLTAGE A term incorrectly used for alternating current. (See Alternating Current)

ALTERNATIONS When a set of variations from one value to a corresponding value has been completed.

ALUMINUM REFLECTOR A reflector (often spherical, parabolic, or ellipsoidal in shape) placed behind the light source in a lighting instrument thus improving the efficiency of the lamp by directing more light rays to the aperture or lens system.

ALZAK A method of treating an aluminum reflector to maintain its reflective surface.

AMBER A type of gelatine used for lighting colors. It is a yellowish-orange transparency used as a color medium for lights. (See Gelatine)

AMBIENT LIGHT A term normally used when working with projection equipment. Ambient light is that light which hits the projection area but is not caused by the projection equipment; e.g., area lighting. Ambient light must be controlled for projection equipment to function at optimum levels.

AMBIENT TEMPERATURE The temperature of the air surrounding any electrical equipment. Most dimmers will state what the ambient temperature of the unit may be for proper performance.

AMMETER A device designed to measure alternating or direct current in amperes.

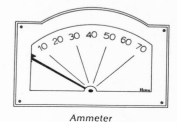
Ammeter

AMPERAGE The number of amperes flowing in a given electrical circuit.

AMPERE (Amp.) A measure of current or rate of flow of electricity; generally associated with capacities of dimmers or fuses. Fuses and breakers are always rated in amps. Fuses and dimmers should never be over-loaded with more watts than they are able to carry; therefore, it is necessary to change an ampere rating to watts, and vice versa, using the following equation:

Watts = Amps x Volts   (P = IE) or   P = Energy available (Watts)
                                          I = Quantity (Amps)
Amps = $\frac{Watt}{Volts}$ (I = $\frac{P}{E}$)   E = Electrical pressure (Volts)

AMPLEX The trade name of a reflector lamp with a colored bulb or lamp. (See Color Bead)

AMPLITUDE The maximum departure of an alternating current or voltage from zero value, measured on either direction from zero point.

AMP TRAP A special fast-action fuse designed to protect rectifiers in silicon controlled rectifier dimmer circuits. Amp Traps should never be replaced with other types of fuses.

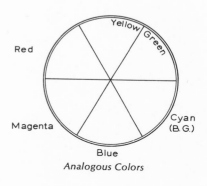
Analogous Colors

ANALOGOUS COLORS Colors which are next to each other on the color wheel.

ANGLE OF INCIDENCE The angle created between the beam of light and the normal line, as it strikes a reflective surface.

ANGLE OF REFLECTION The angle created between the reflected beam and the normal line. The angle of reflection would be the same as the angle of incidence.

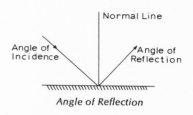
Angle of Reflection

ANGSTROM A measurement of light wave length; 1/10,000 of a micron. Most people see from 4,000 to 7,000 angstroms. Red wave lengths are long while blue wave lengths are short.

ANNEALING A process by which wire has been heated close to the melting point and then permitted to cool slowly. This usually lowers the temper or tensile strength of the wire.

7

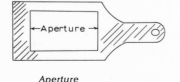

Aperture

ANODE The positive terminal of an electric source; the terminal through which current enters, as opposed to the negative terminal called the "cathode." Used in carbon arc lights. (See Cathode)

A.N.S.I. Abbreviation for the American National Standards Institute, an independent organization which sets standards for comparisons of equipment and materials produced by different manufacturers.

APERTURE The opening, usually in the metal plate, which is between the reflector and the lens system to limit the stray light coming from the reflector.

A.Q.L. Acceptable Quality Level.

ARC A spark between two live wires or connectors. Poor wiring connections sometimes arc and cause fires. All permanent wiring should be soldered and taped, first with rubber tape and then with friction tape or with a plastic electrical tape.

ARC, CONTROLLED A prolonged electrical discharge through air or other gas such as xenon, which produces a high kelvin light source.

ARC LIGHT A spotlight that has for its source an electric current arcing between two carbon rods. It is used for long throws and is usually operated on dc current provided by a rectifier.

ARGON An inert gas often used in incandescent lamps.

ARMATURE In an electromagnetic device such as a generator it is the moving element (a laminated iron core) which creates the magnetic field.

ARRESTER A device placed in a power line to control sudden surges in voltage.

ARTIFICIAL GROUND A grounding electrode; i.e., a metal pipe or rod buried in the earth and connected to a conductor.

ASBESTOS A silicate of calcium and magnesium which is non-combustible and non-conductive. It is often used as an insulator for wires leading into a light instrument.

AUTOMATIC CIRCUIT BREAKER (See Circuit Breaker)

AUTOTRANSFORMER A type of dimmer which is based on the principle of varying intensity by varying the voltage delivered to the equipment. It consists of a soft iron core wrapped with copper wire to form a single coil. The size of the wire and amount of core determine the capacity of the dimmer. A rotating arm containing a carbon brush makes contact either on the coil or on taps from the

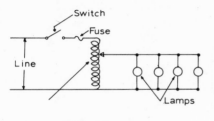

Autotransformer

coil. The coil is placed in series with the input (line), and the brush and one side of the line are placed in series with the output (load). The current requirement for operation is almost negligible.

A.W.G. American Wire Gage. A method of specifying wire diameter. #12 A.W.G. wire is capable of handling 20 amps, while #14 A.W.G. can handle only 15 amps. The higher the number of the wire gage, the smaller the wire.

B

B & S GAUGE The wire gauge used in the United States to specify wire sizes. The abbreviation stands for Brown and Sharp.

BABY SPOT Originally developed as a compact, low-wattage spotlight, using a plano-convex lens and a small spherical reflector. Small theatres use baby spots as area lights from first pipe or beam. Larger theatres use them for backing lights, proscenium lights (tormentor lights), and effects where compactness is essential. Baby spots are designed to use 100-, 250-, or 400-watt lamps. They have an effective throw of approximately 15 feet, and a good focusing device from narrow beam (4 feet in diameter) to wide beam (10 feet in diameter) in a 10-foot throw. Lenses are usually under 5 inches in diameter.

BACKING LIGHT Any instrument used to light a backing. Any light projected through an opening from off stage.

BACKLASH The free play in the gears driving a potentiometer.

Backlash

BACK LIGHTING A method of lighting in which a light is mounted in back of the actor rather than in front. The results tend to highlight the actor's head and shoulders. It is similar to top lighting.

BAFFLE A piece of metal used in lighting instruments to prevent escape of light through ventilating holes.

BALANCED LINE An equal load placed on the hot legs at a power source is said to produce a "balanced" line.

BALCONY LIGHTS Spotlights, usually of 500- to 2,000-watt capacity, mounted on a balcony rail. The balcony angle of 10 to 30 degrees is generally too flat for best results. However, balcony lights are widely used because of convenience or because of lack of better facilities.

BALLAST A resistance wired in series with an arc light, used to control the flow of current through electrodes.

BANK A term often used for a group of dimmers.

BARE CONDUCTOR A conductor with no insulation around it.

Barndoors

BARNDOORS Devices consisting of two or four hinged metal flaps that are placed in front of a spotlight to reduce the beam spread in one or more directions. Often used on Fresnel lights.

BASE-LOAD In a direct current converter, the current which must be taken from the base to keep the unit in a saturated state.

BASES Metal portions of lamps which fit into a socket. Also, weighted plates used to support steel pipes for light trees or light stands.

BATTEN Pipe permanently or semipermanently tied to lines from a grid and used as a light mount. (Most C-clamps for mounting lighting equipment on battens are designed for 1¼-inch or 1½-inch pipe.)

BATTERY OF LIGHTS One or more banks of lights, usually spotlights, used to obtain great intensities. Generally used for large-scale extravaganzas or outdoor staging.

BATTLE SHORT A switch which is activated in case of a short circuit and which sets off a warning light or buzzer.

BAYONET BASE A lamp base (usually for small wattage lamps) with two projections on opposite sides of a smooth cylindrical base.

BEAM The cone of light from a reflector, lens, or spotlight.

BEAM LIGHTING Lighting with spotlights from the beam positions over the audience. The first beam is nearest to the proscenium.

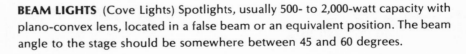

BEAM LIGHTS (Cove Lights) Spotlights, usually 500- to 2,000-watt capacity with plano-convex lens, located in a false beam or an equivalent position. The beam angle to the stage should be somewhere between 45 and 60 degrees.

Beam Projector

BEAM PROJECTOR (Parabolic Spotlight; Sun Spot) A light instrument modeled after the "search light" which used a carbon arc as a light source. The beam projector uses a parabolic reflector. It gives a strong beam of light but it may not be adjusted or focused well. When flooded, it leaves large rings with little or no light in them.

BELL TRANSFORMER A small transformer which converts 120-volts ac and delivers selected voltages such as 6, 12, and 18. It gets its name from the fact that it is often used for doorbells.

BIPOST BASE A two-pronged base used in spotlights. It is available in mini, medium, and mogul bipost sizes. Bipost bases give positive orientation of filament to optical system.

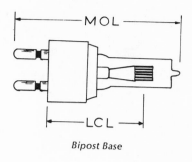

Bipost Base

BLACK BOX (Black Body) A term often used for any piece of equipment where the input and the output are of importance but how it functions is not known to the operator.

BLACK LIGHT (Ultraviolet Light) Light rays, invisible to the human eye, which cause certain fluorescent colors and materials to glow in the dark. Color filters that cut out all rays except ultraviolet are available for high-powered spotlights. Ultraviolet frequencies are higher than those of visible light. Ultraviolet frequencies are about 3,000 to 4,000 angstroms.

BLACK OUT A sudden adjustment of the lights to total darkness, often accomplished by using a master switch.

BLAKE STAPLE A staple, approximately ¾-inch long with insulation at the top. It is often used to fasten lightweight cable; i.e., zipcord, to wood.

BLENDING LIGHT Light which is used to reduce the shadows created by directional light. It permits the actor to come closer to a wall without throwing a strong shadow on it. It also reduces the effect of key lights and so must be used with care.

BLINDER A device used to control the beam spread of light.

BLOW (See Blowout)

BLOWER An electric fan used to cool some types of dimming equipment and instrument lamps.

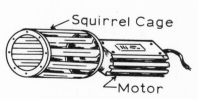

Blower

BLOWOUT The melting of a fuse link because of a short circuit or an overload in an electrical circuit.

BOOKS Any of several types of devices used in spotlights to change colors by remote control or manual operation.

BOOMERANG (Color Boomerang) A box containing color media mounted in front of a light instrument. These media may be changed electrically from the projection box.

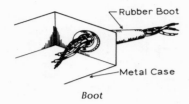

Boot

BOOT A resilient material often placed around wires which enter a dimmer console or powertable control unit. It prevents dust and moisture from entering the unit.

BORDER LIGHTS (Toning Lights) A metal container for lamps which should be mounted above the acting area. It should extend approximately 2/3 the width of the proscenium and should be divided into three circuits for proper color control. Three basic types which are available are: open trough, compartmentalized, and roundel.

BOUNCE LIGHT The light which is reflected off a diffused surface, such as a floor or scenery, causing a soft, indirect light.

BOX LIGHT A simple light with reflector sides and a color frame but no lens. It incorporates a "spread reflection" reflector surface and is used for general illumination.

BRANCH CIRCUIT The final electrical circuit protected by the lowest amperage fuse or breaker.

BRANCH CIRCUIT That portion of an electrical circuit extending beyond the final overcurrent device protecting the circuit.

BREAKOVER VOLTAGE The voltage in which an SCR changes from a non-conductive to a conductive state.

BREASTING A term used when an electrical batten is moved downstage or upstage with ropes which are then tied off on some stable object.

BRIDGE A narrow catwalk just upstage of the proscenium arch. It serves the same purpose as the first electrical batten.

BRIGHTNESS The degree of light given on stage which can be measured. The brightness of lights is measured in foot candles. (See Candle Power)

BROAD A term sometimes used to indicate a wide-angle light instrument.

BROWN OUT A condition caused by the lowering of the voltage due to a consumption rate higher than can be provided. Lamps do not give the proper intensity and other equipment having safety circuits may shut off because of the lowered voltage. Equipment not provided with safety circuits will overheat because of the increased amperage.

BRUSH A piece of conductive material, often graphite, used to take current of different voltages from the coils of a dimmer.

BUCK A condition which exists when an electrical current is held back by magnetic force such as the force created in an autotransformer dimmer or transformer. (See E.M.F.)

BULB Technically it is the glass portion of a lamp; commonly, the lamp in a lighting unit or fixture.

BUS BAR A metal bar inside an electrical steel cabinet to which a tap-off cable might be connected. A "neutral" bus bar is for the connection of the common wire, while the "hot" bus bar is for the hot wire.

BUTTON UP The total shutting down of a piece of equipment for safe keeping.

B-X A brand name for flexible electrical conduit; often used for all flexible conduit.

B-X

BYPASS It is used to describe a temporary shunt circuit around a section of permanent circuit.

C

CABLE Stage wire which is insulated, usually by a rubber covering. It is often composed of multi-stranded copper wire.

CABLE CORE The center of a cable, or the wire under the insulator.

CABLE FILLER Material used in multi-conductor cable to occupy the spaces formed by the assembly of the insulated conductors.

CABLE SHEATH The protective outside cover of a stage cable, often made of heavy rubber or neoprene.

CALCIUM LIGHT (Limelight) An intense white light created by directing an oxyhydrogen flame against a piece of lime.

CALIBRATION A system of placing numbers on dimmers or potentiometers to facilitate the recording of accurate readings of light or sound intensities.

CANDELABRA, ELECTRICAL A socket or base for a lamp slightly smaller than standard.

CANDLE POWER The measurement of luminous intensity; the brightness which is produced on a white surface by one candle placed one foot away from the surface.

CAPACITANCE The phenomenon whereby a circuit stores electrical energy. This storage is obtained through the use of two conducting materials separated by an insulating material; when materials are set up in this manner, they are called capacitors or condensers.

CAPACITOR (See Capacitance)

CAPCOLITE A trade name for a Fresnel light.

CARBON ARC LIGHT (See Arc Light)

CARBON MONOXIDE An odorless gas which emits from the burning of carbon rods. It is associated with the carbon arc lamp and areas where these lamps are used should be well ventilated.

CARBON TETRACHLORIDE A cleaning fluid used to clean contact buttons and brushes of dimmers.

CARTRIDGE FUSE A fuse shaped like a cylinder. Fuses of more than 30 amps are generally cartridge types.

CATHODE The negative electrode or conductor through which electricity leaves equipment. (See Anode)

C-CLAMP "C"-shaped clamp with a single bolt for tightening. C-clamps are used on lighting equipment to fasten the equipment to pipe battens or standards.

CEILING LIGHTS (See Beam Lights)

CHASER LIGHTS Lights which are so wired that each lamp goes on and off in a consecutive manner. This gives the impression that one light turns on the next, or that the lights are moving on a given path.

CHIEF ELECTRICIAN (Electrician) The person in charge of the electrical preparation and operation of a show.

CHROMA The intensity and pureness of a color when compared to the Munsell system. White, black, and gray do not have any chroma.

CHROMACITY The condition of the purity of a color. (See Chroma)

CHROMATIC ABERRATION A condition which produces colored rings, rainbows, or lens leaks emanating from spotlights. They are caused by unequal refractive powers of the lens or reflector. This condition may be corrected by diffusing the light beam with a frost gelatine or by using a no-color gel.

CINNEBACH PROJECTOR A simple light, usually of high intensity, around which a plastic sheet may be fastened. The sheet may be painted with some visual representation, often using Rosco dyes.

CIRCUIT BREAKER (Breaker Switch) A device used in place of a fuse. It opens automatically if the circuit is shorted or overloaded. The circuit can be closed again by pushing a reset button or by turning a switch from the "off" to the "on" position.

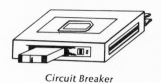

Circuit Breaker

CIRCUIT, ELECTRICAL The complete path of a current from source to load and back to source.

CIRCUIT VOLTAGE The greatest effective difference of potential between any two conductors in an electrical circuit.

CLIP TERMINAL A fastener with spring and jaws, used as a temporary electrical contact for a terminal.

CODE A reference to the national electrical code book or local city laws regarding electrical safety.

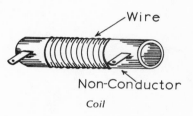

Coil

COIL Thin, insulated wire wrapped around a metal core, such as is used in autotransformer dimmers.

COLLECTOR LENS A lens used in front of the objective lens. The collector lens shortens the focal length of the lens system.

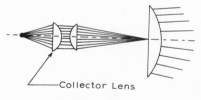

Collector Lens

COLLECTOR RING (See Slip Ring)

COLOR A term normally used to describe the wavelengths from 4,000 to 7,000 angstroms. The eye responds to these wavelengths by translating them as colors. 4,000 angstroms are translated as blue while the longer wavelength of 7,000 angstroms is translated as red. The term "color" is often used in relationship with such terms as "hue," "saturation," and "brightness."

COLOR BEAD The trade name for a reflector lamp with a colored bulb. (See Amplex)

COLOR CODE The identification of wires by the color of the insulator. Generally green is used for ground, white for common or neutral, and black and red for hot circuits.

COLOR FILTER The material used to selectively transmit certain colors. The material may be gelatin, glass, plastic, or cellophane.

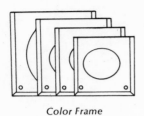

Color Frame

Color Wheel

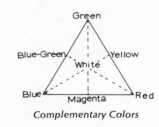

Complementary Colors

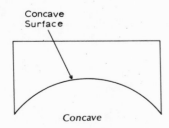

Concave

COLOR FRAME A metal frame used to hold gelatines in front of a lighting instrument. (See Gel Frame)

COLOR MEDIA A general term used to include gelatine (gel), plastic, or glass when they are used to control the visible color in a light beam. (See Absorption Filter)

COLOR PRIMARIES (See Primary Colors)

COLOR TEMPERATURE A term used to describe the degrees of white light given off by a lamp. The color temperature is rated in degrees Kelvin. A warm white light may be 2,600 degrees Kelvin while a whiter light may be 3,200 degrees Kelvin with less red present. Lamps reaching 8,500 degrees Kelvin are available.

COLOR WHEEL A metal wheel fitted with different gel colors which may be rotated by motor or hand. It is used to create flashes of color on the stage. Also: A surface painted with the spectral and non-spectral hues which would include the primary, secondary, and tertiary colors.

COMMON WIRE The same wire as the neutral wire. In a three-wire system this wire should not be fused.

COMMUTATION The changing of alternating current to direct current.

COMMUTATOR Brass segments insulated from each other and mounted on the central shaft of a generator or motor. Brushes ride on the commutator to remove or induce an electrical current.

COMPANY SWITCH An auxiliary electrical switch found in theatres that cater to road shows carrying their own lighting equipment. It is capable of supplying up to 2,600 amps of ac current.

COMPARTMENTALIZED LIGHTS Border lights, footlights, and strip lights have separate compartments for each lamp and are usually equipped with color frames.

COMPLEMENTARY COLORS Any pair of colors in the additive system which combine to make white. These colors will be opposite each other in the color triangle; e.g., blue and yellow.

COMPLIANCE VOLTAGE The consistent voltage of a power supply.

COMPOSITE CONDUCTOR Consists of two or more strands of different metals assembled and operating in parallel.

CONCAVE A surface which is curved inward.

CONCENTRATED FILAMENT A filament which attempts to create a point source of light, thus improving the lamp for use with a lens system.

CONCERT BORDER A term sometimes used to indicate the strip lights on the first light batten.

CONDENSER (See Capacitance)

CONDENSER LENS A lens which brings light rays together. Some lighting instruments use a condenser lens to move the focal point away from the light source in order to eliminate the filament shadow.

CONDUCTIVITY The ability of a material to permit the flow of electricity.

CONDUCTOR Any material (copper, aluminum, iron, silver, etc.) that permits electrons to be easily detached thus allowing electricity to "flow" with little energy lost to heat.

CONDUIT Usually a tubular metal raceway for holding electrical wires.

CONNECTION, ELECTRICAL A splice or union of wires.

CONNECTOR A mechanical device which joins two electrical cables.

CONNECTOR PIN (Slip Connector) An electrical plug and receptacle particularly suited for stage use because of its flat, rectangular design. It doesn't roll. It is available in 20-, 30-, 60-, and 100-amp sizes. Theatres usually use 20-amps.

CONSOLE The manual control portion of a remote-controlled lighting board. It is normally composed of a number of potentiometers mounted in a desk and positioned in such a way as to give full view of the acting area.

CONSTANT CURRENT Electrical current which does not fluctuate below or above set levels for a given piece of equipment.

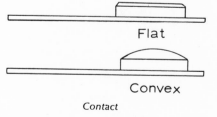

Flat

Convex

Contact

CONTACT The current-carrying part of a switch that is connected or disconnected to open or close an electrical circuit.

CONTACT ARC The spark which is caused when two electrical contacts are brought together or separated. In time this will cause pitting of the contacts and they will need to be replaced.

CONTACT GAP The adjustable space necessary between two contacts in order to stop the flow of electricity.

CONTINUITY TESTERS, ELECTRICAL Any number of devices used to detect a break in a circuit.

CONTINUOUS DUTY A requirement of service which entails operation under a constant load for an indefinite period of time.

CONTROL BOARD A framework which contains fuses, switches, and dimmers necessary to control or adjust stage light intensities.

CONTROL CABLE Usually an assembly of several small conductors taking low voltage current to remote control switches, dimmers, or other equipment.

CONTROLLER A device which serves to govern the electrical power delivered to some piece of equipment.

CONVEX A surface which is curved outward, as in a plano-convex lens.

CONVEX LENS (Plano) A lens which is plane (flat) on one side and convex on the other. The convex lens gives a sharp-edged light which is ideal for beam, booth, and balcony positions.

COOKIE A word derived from the term "Cucalorus." A cookie is a metal insert in a lighting instrument such as an ellipsoidal reflector, to project a simple pattern on the stage floor or stage scenery. The term "Gobo" is sometimes used incorrectly to describe this.

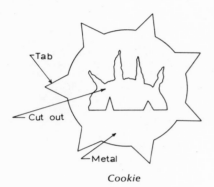

Cookie

COOL COLORS Colors which generally include wavelengths from 4,000 to 5,500 angstroms. These would encompass the blues and greens, combinations of which are often used.

CORD A small, lightweight, and very flexible cable. There is no really sharp dividing line in the definition between cord and cable; but usually cord will be used for lighter weight electrical wires and usually highly flexible stranded wires; i.e., patch cords.

CORE The soft iron center of an autotransformer dimmer which is used because of the magnetic field created by the wire which is wound around it.

COULOMB'S LAW Electrically charged wires of dissimilar charges tend to attract each other and similar charges tend to repulse each other. This law is demonstrated in the rattle or hum of electrical wires which are bundled together by types in the raceways.

COVE LIGHTS (See Beam Lights)

CRADLE A metal frame in first border position on which baby spots are mounted.

CRESCENT WRENCH The trade name for an adjustable wrench. (See Adjustable Wrench)

CROSS-CONNECTING PANEL (See Plugging Panel)

CROSS LIGHTING A condition which exists when two light instruments are focused on the actor, one from the left and one from the right. It is often associated with the McCandless method of lighting.

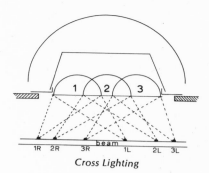
Cross Lighting

CUCALORUS (See Cookie)

CUE SHEET A sheet indicating the various readings or settings of dimmers for a certain scene.

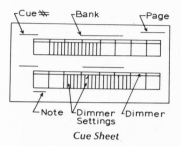
Cue Sheet

CURRENT The movement of electrons through a conductor. Current is measured in amperes.

CYCLE A change in an alternating wave from zero to a positive peak down through zero to a negative peak and back to zero. Two successive alternations in alternating current going from one maximum value to the next one, at which point the current is directed in the same way.

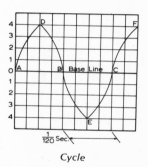
Cycle

CYCLORAMA A large cloth or rigid backdrop which may be flat or curved often used to reflect lighting effects. Cycloramas are often light blue or blue grey.

D

DEAD A term used to indicate that there is no electrical continuity in the wire; the charge of the wire equals that of the ground wire.

DEAD FRONT A switchboard or panel having no exposed wires or parts carrying a current. All switchboards should be dead front.

DEAD SHORT (See Short Circuit)

DEAD SPOT An improperly lighted acting area; the illumination is uneven.

DELTA CONNECTION This connection produces a three-phase or four-wire electrical system where the terminals are so connected to the transformer as to create a triangle like the Greek letter delta. In a Delta connection the first two hot legs (A & B) produce 120 volt to ground and 220 volt to each other. The third leg (C) produces 180 to 190 volts to ground and should not be used for 120 volt purposes.

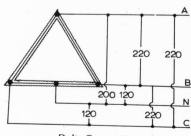
Delta Connection

DEMAND FACTOR The ratio of the maximum demand of the system, or part of the system, to the total connected load of that system under consideration; i.e., the maximum watts used at any time divided by the total wattage of all equipment connected to the system.

DIFFRACTION The process of having a beam of light pass through a substance which causes it to change direction.

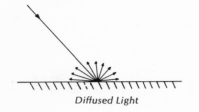
Diffused Light

DIFFUSE A source or surface which breaks up light beams into multiple light rays causing a smooth and even distribution of light.

DIFFUSED LIGHT Light which is spread over a wide area. Shadowless or nearly shadowless light is produced by floods, border lights, footlights, or mediums used to disperse light. Frost gelatine is widely used to diffuse light from spotlights, etc.

DIFFUSED REFLECTOR Any surface which completely disperses a beam of light; e.g. a flat latex painted surface.

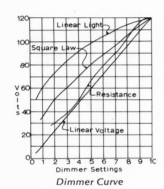
Dimmer Curve

DILUTE PRIMARIES A term used to describe the secondary colors.

DIM To raise or lower the voltage in a lamp thus changing the light intensity.

DIMMER CURVE The wattage output rating of a dimmer related to the level setting of the control unit. Often dimmer voltages increase more rapidly on lower settings and decrease on higher settings.

DIMMER ROOM The room where the dimmers are located.

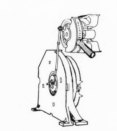
Autotransformer Dimmer

DIMMERS Any number of devices that control intensities of stage lights. Most widely used have been the resistance and autotransformer, but the most versatile dimmers are the magnetic amplifier and the electronic types such as the silicon controlled rectifiers. (See S.C.R.)

DIMMERS, MASTER Any number of devices used to gang a group of dimmers to a single control; e.g., Group Master, Grand Master, Electrical Master.

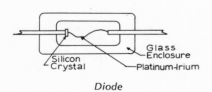
Diode

DIODE A device which has two terminals permitting electricity to flow more easily in one direction than in the other direction.

DIP A term often used to indicate that there is a lower voltage level in the curve of a dimmer than is found either above or below that setting.

DIP IN INTENSITY Involuntary lowering of the intensity of stage lights. It is usually caused by dimmers while fading from one scene to another.

DIP, LAMP A lacquer used to color light bulbs. (See Lamp Dip)

DIRECT BEAM A term used to describe lensless projection equipment for casting a shadow or translucency on a screen.

DIRECT CURRENT The flow of electrons from negative to positive is a continuous, non-fluctuating pattern as opposed to alternating current. (See Alternating Current)

DIRECTIONAL LIGHT (Key Light) A condition said to exist when the audience can clearly see the direction of the light source because of the sharp shadows which it causes.

DIRECT LIGHT Light which comes to the observer directly rather than by reflection from another surface.

DISPERSION Said to occur when a light beam passes through a prism or lens and breaks into its primary and secondary colors.

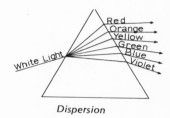

Dispersion

DIVITRIFICATION The appearance of small, superficial cracks or etchings on the surface of a quartz lamp envelope.

DOUBLE POLE SWITCH A switch designed for both sides of an electrical line. It has an "on" and "off" position.

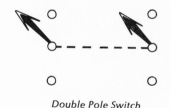

Double Pole Switch

DOUBLE THROW SWITCH A switch designed for both sides of an electrical line. It has two "on" and two "off" positions.

DOUSER A cut-off device in an arc light or follow spot. It is used between a light source and a lens to black out by cutting the beam of light.

DOWN LIGHT A light which is focused down onto the actor. It is often used to create highlights around the actor's head. Such a highlight is not as apparent with frontal lighting.

DOWNSTAGE The area of the stage nearer to the audience. The term is also used to indicate the movement towards the audience from any area of the stage. (See Upstage)

DOWN TIME The amount of time a piece of equipment is not functioning properly.

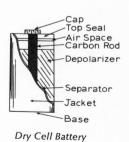

Dry Cell Battery

DRY CELL BATTERY A cell with an immobilized electrolyte which generates voltage. Generally, the positive electrode is made of carbon while the negative electrode is made of zinc and placed in an electrolyte of sal ammoniac paste.

DUPLEX A double receptacle, usually able to accept two male blade or Edison plugs.

DYNA-BEAM SPOTLIGHT A name for a high intensity, incandescent follow spot.

DYNAMO A machine which converts mechanical energy into electrical energy or electrical energy into mechanical energy by using electromagnetic induction.

E

EARTH A term sometimes used for ground.

EDISON BASE The standard screw base often used for household light bulbs.

EFFECTS MACHINE Any instrument which projects multiple slides and/or moving pictures to create an effect.

EFFICACY The capability of a piece of equipment to produce the effect for which it was intended. The term "luminous efficacy" is sometimes used to indicate the effectiveness of a lamp.

EFFICIENCY The ability to produce the desired effect. Often in theatre lights it is related to the amount of energy absorbed and the amount of lumens generated.

ELECTRIC Anything which is operated by or functions through the use of electricity.

ELECTRIC A term often used to describe a light batten; i.e., "first electric" would be the first light batten upstage of the proscenium arch.

ELECTRICAL TAPE Any non-conductive tape which may be wrapped around bare electrical wires where they have been joined. Friction tape was popular but has now been replaced mainly by plastic tape.

ELECTRICIAN'S PLOT (Light Plot) The lighting designer's layout showing stage areas and mounting positions of all instruments used to light the production.

ELECTRICITY It is the flow of electrons through a conductor. The pressure of electricity is measured in volts (usually between 100 and 200 volts). An ampmeter measures the flow of electricity in amperes (amps) per second. Electricity horsepower is subdivided into watts, with 746 watts being equal to 1 horsepower. The unit measure of electrical resistance is stated in ohms.

ELECTRODE Either pole or terminal of an electric apparatus.

ELECTROLYTE A term used for that material in which the conduction of electricity is accompanied by chemical action. Usually, such material is made to break up into ions and thus make it capable of conducting an electrical current more readily.

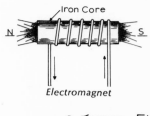

Electromagnet

ELECTROMAGNET A magnet which functions only when an electrical force is passed through the windings around an iron core.

ELECTRON A negatively charged particle which surrounds a positively charged nucleus. Electricity is created when these electrons have been removed from the nucleus and then returned to the nucleus.

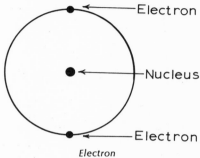

Electron

ELECTRONIC A term used regarding equipment which functions due to the passing of free electrons through semi-conductors, gas, or vacuum tubes. The term electric differs in that it concentrates on the movement of electrons through metal conductors.

ELECTRONIC FLASH (See Strobe Light)

ELLIPSOIDAL REFLECTOR A reflector with two focal points. Ellipsoidal reflectors extend further around the lamp than parabolic reflectors and so capture more light rays, directing them to a second conjugate focal point.

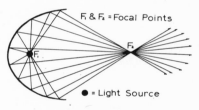

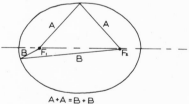

Ellipsoidal Reflector

ELLIPSOIDAL SPOTLIGHT A spotlight which combines shutter systems and lenses to increase intensity and to frame light to give a pattern. Ellipsoidal spotlights are particularly valuable as beam, balcony, or booth lights where beams must be cut to proscenium edge.

EMBRYO SPOT (Inky) A term used to refer to small spotlights used extensively in photographic studios. However, they are very useful on stage in small quarters such as telephone booths or fireplaces.

E.M.F. Abbreviation for Electromotive Force. It is the force created by the flow of current throughout wire because of an overabundance of electrons. Transformers function as they do because of the back EMF created by the coil and which restricts the flow of power.

Ellipsoidal Spotlight

EMITTER CLOTH A cotton cloth soaked in varnish and used to separate or insulate electrically charged wires or parts.

E.M.T. Electrical metal tubing abbreviation, often called conduit.

ENVELOPE The glass bulb around a filament which prevents the oxygen environment from coming in contact with the filament.

F

FADE IN (Sneak, Steal) The gradual dimming up of stage lights.

FADE OUT (Sneak, Steal) The gradual dimming out of stage lights.

FADER The dimmer which controls the voltage output of two separate presets in a remote control light board.

FARAD A unit of capacitance. A condenser or capacitor will have the capacitance of one Farad if the voltage across it is increased one volt; its stored electrical energy is increased by one coulomb.

FEEDER Any conductor of an electrical system between the main switchboard and the branch circuit over-current protecting device.

FEEDER CABLE The heavy gauge cable (often 000 gauge) used to connect a portable dimmer to an electrical source of high amperage potential.

FEED LINE, ELECTRICAL The conductor delivering power to equipment.

FEMALE PLUG, ELECTRICAL (Body) A device containing one or more receptacles.

FIBER OPTICS A number of transparent glass fibers bundled together and with the ability to transmit light around corners with relatively little loss in light intensity.

FILAMENT The part of a lamp, usually made of tungsten, which causes sufficient resistance to the flow of electricity to produce enough heat for incandescence to result. Concentrated filaments made possible the use of lenses because the light source became closer to being a single point.

FILAMENT IMAGE A projection of filament shadow from the lens of a spotlight. It may be corrected by widening the focus of the spotlight through an adjustment or by diffusing with a frost gelatine.

FILL LIGHT Non-directional or multi-directional light. This creates soft shadows, as in general illumination.

FILLER (See Cable Filler)

FILTER A color medium placed in front of a light, or a perforated piece of metal (strainer), used in front of spotlights to filter concentration without changing color value.

FIXTURE A term sometimes used to indicate a light instrument. It is more often used by non-theatre personnel than by theatre technicians.

FLAG (See Gobo) ·

FLASHOVER The condition existing when an insulator breaks down because of external damage or because of a sudden increase in voltage above the rating of the insulator. Flashover causes an electrical discharge through the air to a differently charged source.

FLASH BULB A lamp filled with an oxygen atmosphere containing metal foil or wire. When electrical power is passed through the wire, it is heated to incandescence and momentarily burns brilliantly in the oxygen atmosphere.

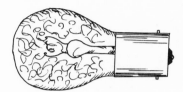

Flash Bulb

FLATTENED ELLIPSOIDAL REFLECTOR Because the filament in a lamp is not actually a light point source, ellipsoidal reflector companies, such as Century, have designed reflectors which have been broken into many small rectangular or circular ridges. The theory is that these ridges will make up for the fact that the lamp does not have a light point source and thus the instrument will have a smoother distribution of light in its beam.

FLIPPER (See Barndoor)

FLOOD LIGHT A term often used for cyclorama lighting or as a concentration of light from a given source. There are two basic types of floodlights: Standing and hanging.

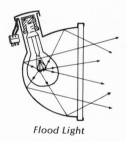

Flood Light

FLOOR PLUG A large plug designed for heavy loads of 20, 30, and 50 amps. It fits into a floor pocket, usually recessed in the stage floor, or into a portable plugging box.

FLOOR POCKET The metal box set flush into the stage floor which houses the receptacles into which stage cables are plugged.

Outlet
Floor Plug

FLOW The movement of electrons through a conductor.

FLUORESCENCE The absorption of light energy by matter when the absorption takes longer than 10 to the 8th power to subsequently give off this same light.

FLUORESCENT LIGHT An instrument that uses a mercury arc to create light, mainly in the ultraviolet range. The energy thus produced activates the phosphors (phosphoric calcium, zinc, etc.) which then emit light visible to the human eye.

FLUX The energy of the lights on a given area. Normally this term is used synonymously with "lumens."

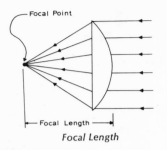

Focal Length

Follow Spot

FLY To lift a light batten, or any other scenery, so that it is supported by ropes or cables.

FOCAL LENGTH The distance from the center of a lens to its focal point, which is the point at which the rays of light converge. The shorter the focal length, the wider the beam of light or the wider the angle of dispersion.

FOCAL POINT The point at which a reflector or lens centralizes or converges all the light rays from the light source.

FOCUS LIGHTS To set positions of spotlights and other lighting equipment. To adjust the distance between lamp and lens, thereby changing the size of the area covered by light. Sharp focus or back focus means narrow beam; wide focus or front focus means wide beam.

F.O.H. Abbreviation for Front of House. The term might be used in describing balcony lights as being FOH lights.

FOLLOW To keep an actor in the spotlight as he moves on the stage. The follow spot light instrument is generally used for this task.

FOLLOW SPOT A light instrument designed to follow the moving actor. It is mounted on a swivel and the lights used are mainly arc or incandescent. Follow spots often have lamps in excess of 1500 watts and have a throw of up to 150 feet.

FOOT-CANDLE A unit of illumination equal to 1 lumen per square foot. It is the amount of light produced by a standard candle at a distance of 1 foot. If the candle power of a given lamp is known, foot-candles at a given distance can be computed from the following equation:

$$\text{FOOT-CANDLES} = \frac{\text{Lumens}}{\text{Area (in square feet)}}$$

FOOTLIGHTS A trough for lights on the stage floor or embedded in the floor immediately in front of the curtain. Footlights are similar to border lights and, in some cases, they are interchangeable. The basic types are "open trough," "compartmentalized," and "roundel."

FOURWIRE SYSTEM A three-phase electrical system which uses three hot legs and one common leg. It may service equipment which has been designed with one more winding, thus requiring a three-phase system. A 220-volt, single phase may be obtained by using two hot legs and the common leg, and 120 volts may be obtained by using one hot leg and the common or neutral wire. Such a system is desirable in any theatre installation because it provides the lighting technician with more power and versatility.

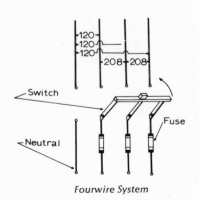

Fourwire System

FREQUENCY The rapidity of alternations; i.e., the number of cycles per second as in 60-cycle alternating current.

FRESNELITE The trade name for a compact spotlight using the Fresnel lens.

FRESNEL LENS A lens which is reduced in thickness by making curved sections into concentric rings and stepping them back toward the plane. This results in a shorter focal length without increasing the thickness of the glass. The lens was developed in 1800 by Augustin Fresnel.

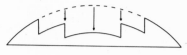

Fresnel Lens

FRESNEL SPOTLIGHT A light instrument which uses a lens thinner than the plano-convex lens. It will therefore withstand greater heat without cracking, making it adaptable to compact housings and higher-wattage lamps. Since a Fresnel lens gives a soft-edged, diffused light, its use is limited to the stage proper. It is best used on the first pipe, tormentor, or on locations behind the proscenium only. The sizes for the Fresnel are 150-, 500-, 750-, 1,000- to 1,500-, 2,000-, 5,000-, and 10,000-watts.

Fresnel Spotlight

FRICTION TAPE A tape or cloth strip impregnated with a moisture-resistant, sticky material which makes the tape non-conductive. The tape is often used to wrap around bare wires which have been joined together.

FRONT PROJECTION The practice of placing an image on a screen or other surface by means of a light instrument. Problems of distortion often arise because the projector must be placed outside the optical axis of the system. Ambient light must be controlled so that the image is intense enough to be seen by the audience.

FROST A translucent gelatine used to diffuse light. It is useful in blending area lights and in softening harsh lines. Frosted lamps are often used in scoops to soften the light edge.

Funnel

FUNNEL (Top Hat) A device designed to control the beam spread of light, to frame given areas, and to keep light from unwanted spilling on stage. It is often used with Fresnel lights.

Fuse

FUSE An electrical conductor in a circuit which melts and breaks the circuit if a current greater than the prescribed load is introduced. It is a protective device.

FUSE HOLDER A device into, or onto, which a fuse may be mounted providing connections for the terminals of the fuse.

Fuse Holder

FUSE PLUG A fuse which generally uses a standard Edison screw base, or a "tamperproof" screw base. It consists of a fuse wire or strip mounted in a porcelain container and has a mica or glass cover for inspection.

Fuse Plug

27

G

GAGE A method of specifying wire diameter. (See A.W.G.)

GATE In an SCR dimmer, the device which fires to control the wave pattern of the alternating current. The voltage is controlled by this system which adjusts the intensity of the lamp.

GANG To plug more than one instrument into a single circuit. This makes individual control of the light instruments impossible.

GAUGE (See Gage)

GEL An abbreviation for "gelatine." It is often used to mean all color media.

GELATINE Thin, transparent sheets made of animal jelly and dye. They are used as color mediums for stage lights. They are generally 20 by 24 inches in size and come in nearly 100 different shades and tints. Their usual life expectancy is 100 hours. The major brands are: Cinemoid, Cinebex, and Roscolene. Gel is not practical when used close to water because it will dissolve.

GEL FRAME The metal frame which holds the gelatine flat in front of the light instrument.

GENERAL ILLUMINATION Footlights, border lights, strip lights, etc., used for toning, blending, and establishing the basic color mood for a play.

GENERATOR, AC The device which removes the negatively charged electrons from the nucleus. Most generators function on a rotary basis and are carefully controlled as to the number of electrons they remove. This, in turn, controls the voltage.

GHOST LIGHT The term derives from an old superstition which suggests leaving a light burning on an empty stage to prevent a ghost from moving into the theatre.

GHOST LOAD (Phantom Load) A lamp or a resistance in an unseen or obscure place on stage which can be connected in parallel with a stage light in order to "load" the dimmer for complete dimouts. Resistance dimmers need ghost loads only if the load they control is less than the rated minimum load of the dimmer.

GLARE (Bounce Light) A light reflection too bright for comfortable vision. It is caused by too light a background or too great a contrast of color in the background.

GOBO An opaque material mounted in front or on the sides of a light instrument to control the light. The term is sometimes used for a circular cookie which narrows the pool of light or which creates a pattern on scenic units.

GRAND MASTER A device which controls all dimmers on a light board including the group master.

GRAPHITE A form of carbon which is a conductor. Because of its lubrication potential, it is often used as brushes on electrical dimmers.

GROUND (Grounding) To connect an electrical system to the path of least resistance. To meet safety regulations, all electrical systems must have a grounded leg plus the common (neutral) and the hot connection.

GROUND BUS The bar to which several grounded wires may be connected in order to tie them into the main ground wire.

GROUNDED OUTLET An outlet which is equipped with one grounded circuit.

GROUP MASTER A device which controls all individual dimmers or switches of a segment on a light board.

GROWLER The instrument used to determine if there are shorts in electromagnetic motors.

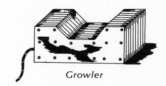
Growler

H

HALOGEN GAS A general name used to describe iodine, fluorine, bromine, and chlorine.

HANG To mount or place a lighting instrument in a desired location.

HANGER The pipe or yoke mounting for a spotlight. The "C" clamp would be at the top.

HARD LIGHT The light produced by a light instrument and which has a clearly defined edge, as opposed to a soft edge which is not clearly defined.

HEAT SINK The aluminum fins often found on electronic dimmers and used to dissipate the heat created by the dimmer.

Hickey

HICKEY A tool commonly used by electricians to bend conduit. Hickies are available in various sizes; i.e. ½", ¾", 1", etc.

H.I.D. LAMP High Intensity Discharge Lamp; i.e., a mercury vapor lamp.

HIGH HAT (See Funnel)

HOT CIRCUIT An electrical circuit carrying a current.

HOT FRONT A term used to describe a light board where the operator could possibly come into physical contact with a 120-volt current. Such light boards fall outside O.S.H.A. safety regulations.

HOT LINE (Live Line, Live Wire) An electrical circuit carrying a potential and usually terminating in a receptacle or panel. It is a leg of line voltage as opposed to the ground or neutral wire.

HOT SPOT A stage area which is brighter or "hotter" than others because of an uneven distribution of light.

HOUSE BOARD A control board which is separate from the main light board and which is capable of operating the house lights and possibly some work lights.

HOUSE LIGHTS Lights used to illuminate the auditorium. Intensity should be adequate for reading programs but never glaring. A level of 10 foot-candles is minimum for auditorium lighting.

HUE The quality of a color which enables it to be distinguished from other colors of the same brilliance.

I

ILLUMINATE To bring light to a given area.

ILLUMINATION The surface light intensity, expressed in foot-candles. The human eye adjusts to intensities of 1 to 10,000 foot-candles. However, brightness above 100 foot-candles is not easily discernible so it is seldom necessary to illuminate any stage over that amount.

IMAGE The pattern of the filament which is shown in the beam of light when the instrument is in complete focus. An ellipsoidal must be kept slightly out of focus so the filament image does not show. (See Filament Image)

IMPEDANCE The resistance which is found in an electrical wire when ac current is massed through it. Impedance is measured in ohms.

INCANDESCENCE The condition obtained when a substance is sufficiently heated to give off light. In an incandescent lamp, when the tungsten filament is heated by the electrical flow through it, it gives off light.

INCANDESCENT LAMP An electrical lamp in which electric current flows through a filament where the resistance is sufficient to cause the filament to glow or incandescent.

INCIDENCE (See Angle of Incidence)

INDEPENDENT Said of a dimmer which is operated individually and not switched into the preset system of a group master.

INDUCTION The electrical resistance created when a conductor is placed within a magnetic field, e.g., in a transformer.

INDUCTOR A coil with or without an iron core which opposes the changes in current due to its self inductance.

INFRA-RED The color above (having a shorter wavelength) the visible red which measures 7,000 angstroms.

INKY A small light instrument having a 100-watt lamp; often used in place of a three-inch Fresnel.

INPUT The current applied to any electrical piece of equipment or to a circuit. The energy or power supplied to a machine for it to produce power. (See Output)

INSTRUMENT The equipment which houses a lamp and which is normally used in theatres. It is synonymous with "luminaire."

INSULATOR Any material which does not permit its electrons to be easily detached; e.g., glass, dry cloth, rubber, air, etc. This material does not permit electricity to flow through it and so can be used to control the location of electricity.

INTENSITY The brightness of light on any given area from any given piece of lighting equipment. Light intensity depends upon the capacity of the lamp, quality of lens and reflector, distance from the stage, and the gelatine used. Also: The degree of purity or saturation of a color. (See Chroma)

INTERCONNECT PANEL (See Patch Board)

INTERLOCK A mechanical device which temporarily ties individual dimmers together so they may be brought up or down as a unit.

INVERSE-SQUARE LAW (See Law of Squares)

IRIS An attachment for a spotlight which will adjust the diameter of a lens aperture to any size from closed to wide open. The primary use of the iris is to control the size of light beams from arc lights or follow spots.

IZENHOUR The trade name for a thyrotron tube light board. Its name derives from its inventor, George Izenhour, of Yale University.

J

JOULE A measure of electrical energy; i.e., the power of one watt for one second, or the work done by forcing one ampere through a resistance of one ohm for one second.

JUICE Jargon used for electrical current.

JUMPER A short piece of wire used to complete a temporary circuit.

JUNCTION BOX An electrical box in which two or more circuits are together. Permanent splices should be made in the junction box.

K

KELVIN SCALE The temperature scale often used in defining lamp color temperature. It has the same divisions as the Centigrade or Celsius scale, but uses a zero point of -273 degrees Centigrade; this is considered to be absolute zero.

KEY LIGHT A highly directional light. It tends to give shadows which show the shape and direction of the light.

KEYBOARD A term sometimes used to refer to a particular type of light switchboard designed for more subtle control of individual areas.

KEYSTONE DISTORTION The distortion creating a picture which is wider on the top than the bottom or vice versa. The effect is often encountered when a slide projector is mounted on a plane different from that of the projection screen.

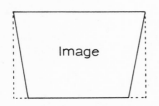

Keystone Distortion

KILL To turn off lights.

KILOWATT A unit of power equal to 1,000 watts. Spotlights are often identified by their kilowatt power; e.g., a 2,000-watt spotlight is often called a 2kw.

KILOWATT HOUR A unit of measurement equal to 1,000 watts expended over a period of one hour. Electricity is sold by the kilowatt hour.

KLEIGLIGHT The trade name of the Kleigl Company for an ellipsoidal reflector. It is often used incorrectly for all ellipsoidals. A high-intensity light using the arc between two carbon electrodes as the light source. Kleiglight is sometimes used as a synonym for any bright light.

KIRCHOFF'S CURRENT LAW The sum of all current flowing in one direction in a given circuit must be equal to the sum of all current flowing in the other direction.

KIRCHOFF'S VOLTAGE LAW The sum of all voltage sources acting in a complete circuit must be equal to the sum of all voltage drops in the circuit.

KNIFE BLADE CONTACT FUSE A fuse often shaped like a cartridge fuse. The ends are flat metal protrusions which make the contact with the fuse holder.

KNIFE SWITCH An open or exposed switch that sandwiches the connecting terminal or connector between two contacts of the source.

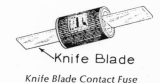

Knife Blade

Knife Blade Contact Fuse

L

LAG The amount of time used for a dimmer to give voltage which was indicated on the sending unit or potentiometer.

LAMBERT A measurement of light equal to one lumen per square centimeter.

LAMINATED CORE The iron core, made up of several layers of insulated metal, forming the basic core of a transformer or armature.

LAMP BASE The metal part of a lamp which fastens the lamp into its fixture. Bases carry such designations as mogul or medium screw base, single recessed contact, medium bipost, medium prefocus, etc.

LAMP DIP The name given to the lacquer used to color light bulbs. The bulbs are dipped briefly while burning. Dipped bulbs are suitable for strip lights, border lights, and older types of footlights. Heat generated by lamps of 100 watts or more causes flaking of the lacquer.

LAMP LIFE The number of hours a lamp functions. Life may range from 10 to 2,000 hours. The housing of the lamp is critical, since the higher the heat in the housing, the shorter the life voltage means a shorter lamp life. Lamp life may also be shortened by rough handling of the lamp.

LAMPS Lighting instruments which are designed for lamps of a given size, shape, wattage, and lamp base. Occasionally, sizes and wattage can be interchanged. The different types of bulbs are: G-type (globular); Par-38, 46, 56, or 64 (parabolic aluminized reflector); P.S. (pear shaped); R-type (reflector); T-type (tubular).

LAW OF MAGNETISM It states that like sources repel each other while unlike sources are attracted to each other. (See Coulomb's Law)

Lamp Base

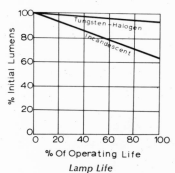

Lamp Life

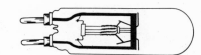

Tubular Lamp Bipost Base

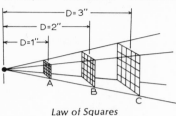

A=1 sq. ft.   Illumination = 1 ft. candle
B=4 sq. ft.   Illumination = ¼ ft. candle
C=9 sq. ft.   Illumination = ⅑ ft. candle

Law of Squares

LAW OF REFLECTION The angle of incidence of any reflected object is equal to its angle of reflection. (See Angle of Reflection)

LAW OF SQUARES It states that light intensity decreases in an inverse proportion to the square of the distance.

L.C.L. (See Light Center Length)

LEAK Said of a condition when light is seen which should not be seen.

LEAKAGE, ELECTRICAL The small electrical loss which occurs because of poor insulation on the wiring.

LEG A section or phase of an electrical system such as a "hot leg" or "hot bus."

LEKOLITE The trade name of the Century Company for an ellipsoidal reflector. It is often used incorrectly for all ellipsoidals.

LENSES The transparent glass or plastic which is ground or cast so that it changes the direction or the angle of the light rays which pass through. Lenses are designated by diameter and focal length, which is the distance from the center of the lens to the point where the light rays converge. Thick lenses have shorter focal lengths. Shorter focal lengths are more desirable for short throws and long focal lengths for long throws.

LENS SIZES The diametrical measurement of lenses. Often light instruments such as ellipsoidal reflectors are named by the dimension of the lens; i.e., a "6 x 9" would be an ellipsoidal reflector having a lens six inches in diameter and with a nine-inch focal length.

LIGHT An electro-magnetic radiation which is visible to the human eye.

LIGHT BATTEN An electrical batten on which lights are hung. It usually has a number of permanent electrical circuits on it. (See Light Bridge)

LIGHT BOARD The controls for the dimmers which are adjusted during the play. These controls may be the remote sending unit and thus the dimmers may be in a different location; or the controls may be part of the dimmers themselves as in an autotransformer dimmer.

LIGHT BRIDGE A catwalk flown just upstage of the proscenium arch. It serves the same purpose as the first electric, or first light batten. (See Light Batten)

LIGHT CENTER LENGTH (LCL) The distance between the lamp filament and the base. This is a critical measurement because it positions the filament or light source in relation to the reflector and the lens system.

LIGHTING COLORS Theoretically, the primary colors of light are red, blue, and

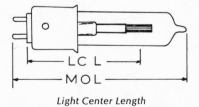

Light Center Length

green and, used in equal intensities, will give white light. Varying intensities of these colors will produce a wide range of colors on stage. The secondary colors of magenta, blue-green, and amber are sometimes used in border lights. Colors for spotlights are usually light pink, light amber, light straw, light blue, light lavender, light gray, and light chocolate. The most flattering and youthful colors are combinations of pink, lavender, and light blue.

LIGHTING CONTROL CONSOLE The panel, often mounted on a desk or table, which contains the controls used to adjust the lighting on stage. For ease of operation, these consoles are placed in the rear of the house for better visibility.

LIGHTING DESIGNER The individual who through compassion, understanding, and creativeness, sets the locations of light instruments to create the effect best suited for the play.

LIGHTING GRID A term often used for the grid above the stage on a thrust or in-the-round stage, from which lights are hung. In a proscenium stage, the light grid would be composed of beams or islands and light battens.

LIGHTING REHEARSAL A rehearsal used by the lighting designer and the director to set light levels and areas before the technical rehearsal. It is a good practice too often ignored.

LIGHTING TEMPLATE A plastic plate with light instruments patterns cut out so that the holes may be used to trace instrument positions on a light plot. Normally, these templates are designed to be in the same scale as the floor plan of the scenic designer.

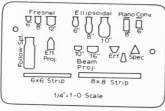

Lighting Template

LIGHT PLOT An informational sheet which indicates the position and type of light instrument to be used, the circuit and dimmer to be used, and the gel color required.

LIGHT PORTAL A tall, narrow slot inside proscenium or auditorium walls, where spotlights can be hung for proper lighting. At a minimum, a good light portal should be 8 feet high and 18 inches wide. It should be at least 6 feet above stage level.

LIGHT SPILL Light which strays from the main beam of a light instrument and falls on parts of the stage where it is not wanted. It can generally be controlled by a gobo, barndoor, louvre, or top hat.

LIGHT TREE A metal pipe placed vertically in some type of base so that light instruments can be mounted on the pipe.

LIMBO A background which does not call attention to itself; black or dark gray are often used.

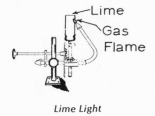

Lime Light

LIME LIGHT An intense white light created by directing an oxyhydrogen flame against a piece of lime. At the proper temperature the lime will incandesce. (See Calcium Light)

LINEAR CURVE In dimming equipment, the curve which is created by an autotransformer dimmer. It gives more control at the lower setting than at the higher. Because of this, settings which are changed from 10% to 20% will show less change in the light than if they were changed from 80% to 90%.

LINE DROP (Loss) The voltage drop or loss which results from the resistance or usage in that line.

LINE, ELECTRICAL The source of power; the "line" side of a circuit as opposed to the "load" side. The feed line is the conductor delivering power to the equipment.

LINE STARTER A motor which has a starter which applies full line voltage to the motor immediately on operation of the starter.

LINE VOLTAGE The voltage at the terminal of a power line system or from a standard wall outlet.

LOBSTERSCOPE A disk attachment for a spotlight; used to produce a flicker of light.

LOUVERS Several black metal strips, often circular, which absorb stray light that doesn't follow the proper angle from the reflector.

LOW NOISE LAMP A lamp which is so constructed that it produces little or no audio interference.

L.P.W. (See Lumen Per Watt)

LUMEN A standard unit of measurement of the rate of flow of light energy. It is the flow of the light through 1 square foot of a sphere having a 1-foot radius and a centered light source of 1 candle power. One lumen of light evenly applied to 1 square foot produces 1 foot-candle (.0015 watt). The formula is:

$$\text{LUMENS} = \text{Foot-Candles} \times \text{Area (in square feet)}$$

LUMEN PER WATT The number of lumens which a light instrument gives off per watt used. The term is often used as a measurement of the efficiency of a lamp.

LUMINAIRE A term used for a light instrument and including all those parts needed to make the instrument function as intended.

LUMINESCENCE The absorption of light energy by any matter (such as phosphoric calcium or zinc) which gives off light without much heat.

LUX The equivalent of 1 candle power under the metric system. It consists of the amount of light produced on one square meter from a light source of one candle.

M

MAGAMP (See Magnetic Amplifier Dimmer)

MAGNET A metal body which has the ability to attract or repel other metal or magnetic materials. Magnets may be permanent, electromagnetic, or natural, such as the loadstone.

MAGNETIC AMPLIFIER DIMMER (Magamp) A dimmer which stacks saturable dimmers to create a dimmer than can control thousands of ac watts. It has no moving parts and creates practically no heat.

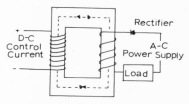

Magnetic Amplifier Dimmer

MAGNETIC CIRCUIT BREAKER A circuit breaker which is actuated when the current produces enough of a magnetic field to actuate a magnetic coil which then opens the contact points. The current rating of such a circuit breaker is determined by the number of turns and wire size of the magnetic coil.

MAGNETIC FIELD The area around a magnet or electromagnet where the magnetic forces may be measured.

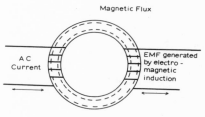

Magnetic Field

MAINTENANCE The adjustments which need to be made on any piece of equipment to keep it, or to bring it back, into full function or service.

MALE PLUG (Cap) An electrical connector that has one or more prongs and is fastened to the "load" (equipment to be used).

MANUAL DIMMER A dimmer which must be physically operated by the lighting technician, not by remote control. Manual dimmers are resistance and autotransformer dimmers.

MANUAL RESET The process of making an adjustment on a dimmer setting within a bank, not through a preset system.

MASTER DIMMER Any one of a number of devices used to gang a group of dimmers to a single control. A group master controls a bank or partial bank of dimmers or switches. A grand master controls all individual dimmers or switches on the board. (See Grand Master and Group Master)

MASTER SWITCH A switch that controls or overrides all other switches.

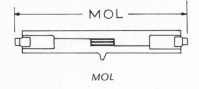

MOL

MAT Said of a surface which is dull or roughened and which diffuses light in a flat reflection.

MAXIMUM OVERALL LENGTH (MOL) The maximum dimension of a lamp from base to tip of envelope. In double-ended lamps, it is the measurement from base to base.

MEDIUM TWO PIN A lamp base, like the medium bipost lamp base which is often used with tungsten-hallogen lamps. The pins are about 3/16-inch in diameter.

MEGAMPERE One million amperes.

MEGAVOLT One million volts.

MEGOHM A resistance of 1,000,000 ohms.

MEMORY SYSTEM A term often used for a light board which is capable of permanently recording level and time settings for light cues. Information may be stored into the memory system by a variety of means: mechanical, magnetic, electrostatic, ferroelectric, etc.

MERCURY SWITCH A silent switch that moves a vial of mercury to make the electrical connection. Mercury switches must be placed in a certain limited position; i.e., vertically, for the unit to function properly.

MERCURY-VAPOR LAMP A lamp which consists of a glass envelope in which a mercury gas is placed. The gas gives off light when the atoms and electrons return to a neutral state after having been excited by a passing electrical current. The gas and its pressure may be varied to change the wavelength of the light produced; e.g., ultraviolet light.

MICROAMPERE One millionth of an ampere.

MICRON A unit of measurement that is 1/1,000 of an inch long. It is used to reduce the fractions of a light wavelength to decimals.

MICROVOLT One millionth of a volt.

MILLIAMPERE One thousandth of an ampere (.001).

MILLIVOLT One thousandth of a volt (.001).

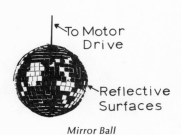

Mirror Ball

MIRROR BALL A three-dimensional object, usually spherical in shape, covered with small mirrors. When a spotlight is focused on it, it throws light images over the audience and the stage. If the ball is rotated, the spots move. Generally the ball is hung in a position which is out of the sight lines of the audience.

MODELING The using of lights to achieve a three-dimensional effect. This is done by using lights of two different colors and having them come from two different sources.

MODELING-LIGHT The light hitting the actor or performer from the opposite side as the key-light.

MOGUL LAMP BASE The next base larger than medium. It is used for higher wattages; e.g., in the bipost-based lamps, those having 1,000 watts or more use a mogul bipost base.

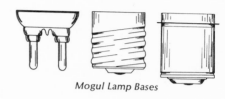

Mogul Lamp Bases

MOL (See Maximum Overall Length, and see Light Center Length)

MULTIPLE A condition existing when two female (line) receptacles are tied to a single male (load) plug.

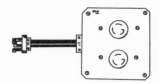

Multiple

MULTIPLE-CONDUCTOR CABLE A combination of two or more individually insulated wires into one cable; i.e., three-conductor cable.

MULTIPLE SERIES The condition when electrical devices are wired in multiples where the devices serve as the electrical path to complete the circuit.

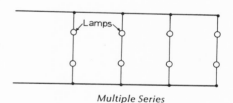

Multiple Series

N

N.E.C. Abbreviation for the National Electrical Code.

NEGATIVE A term used to describe the electrical pole which has an excess of electrons. Electrons flow from the negative terminal to the positive pole. Opposite of positive.

NEON LAMP A glass envelope which is filled with neon gas and which contains two or more electrodes. At the proper voltage, generally above 90 volts, the gas ionizes and permits the arc to move between the electrodes.

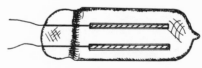

Neon Lamp

NEON LIGHT Light which is created by forcing electricity through a certain gas at a given pressure and temperature. The gas then becomes a conductor and will glow. The color may be varied by changes in pressure, temperature, and type of gas.

NEUTRAL DENSITY FILTER A filter which reduces all light wavelengths equally; i.e., frosted gel, thus dimming down the light.

NEUTRAL WIRE The common or ground wire in electricity.

NOBLE GAS A general term used for such inert gases as xenon, argon, helium, etc. These gases are often used inside the glass envelopes of lamps.

NO-COLOR GEL Gelatine which contains very little color. It may be purchased under such names as no-color blue, no-color pink, etc.

NOMINAL IMPEDANCE The impedance normally found in a circuit under normal operating conditions.

NON-CONDUCTOR An insulating material which is highly resistant to the free flow of electrons.

NON-DIM CIRCUIT An electrical circuit which is not directed through a dimmer board.

NON-DIRECTIONAL LIGHT (Fill Light) A method of lighting which creates little or no shadows.

NON-LENS SPOTLIGHTS Light instruments which have only a reflector and a light source; e.g., scoops, olivettes.

NON-SPECTRAL HUES A mixture of separate wavelengths which the human eye recognizes as colors. Colors which may be distinguished by the human eye, need not appear on the spectrum. For example, magenta is a non-spectral hue. It is made by overlapping the blue and red wavelengths of the spectrum.

NORMAL LINE The line which is perpendicular to the reflective surface. If the surface is round, then the line will be perpendicular to the tangent of the curve.

NORMAL MODE The orthodox condition or method of operation of a piece of equipment.

NO-VOLTAGE RELEASE A switch held closed by an electromagnet which is released or opened at a pre-determined minimum voltage.

O

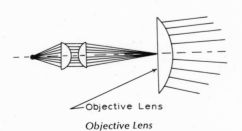

Objective Lens

OBJECTIVE LENS The final lens in a lens system. It is the lens which is closest to the object.

OHM The unit of electrical resistance. It is the value of the resistance one volt will maintain in a current of one ampere.

OHM'S LAW The equation for determining voltage (E), amperage (I), or resistance (R) when only two of the factors are known:

$$E = IR \qquad I = \frac{E}{R} \qquad R = \frac{E}{I}$$

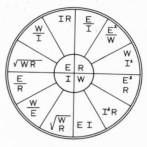

Ohm's Law

OLIVETTE A box-shaped floodlight. Its flat reflective surfaces do not make it as efficient as the scoop flood light which uses an ellipsoidal or parabolic reflector. (See Non-Lens Spotlights)

OPAQUE Said of any material which does not permit light rays to pass through.

OPEN CIRCUIT An electrical circuit which has not been completed. This often occurs when a switch has not been closed and thus the normal flow of electrons is stopped.

OPEN WIRING Insulators which are supported only by knobs or cleats or other insulators but without any other type of covering or enclosure.

OPTICAL AXIS A straight line drawn from the center of the reflector through the center of the filament and the center of the lens.

Olivette

OSHA The Occupational Safety and Health Administration. It is an arm of the Federal Government which enforces safety regulations.

OUTLET A permanent electrical installation to which equipment can be attached; the line (outlet) as opposed to the load (equipment) which is plugged into the outlet.

OUTPUT The useful energy or power delivered by a given machine as opposed to the input or energy supplied to the machine.

OUTPUT CURVE The adjustment which can be made on a dimmer in accordance with the existing voltage at any particular setting. The Linear or Square Law curves are often used.

OUTPUT STAGE The terminal or final stage of any piece of electronic equipment.

OVAL BEAM A spotlight with a special Fresnel lens designed to throw an oval rather than a round beam.

OVERLOAD A CIRCUIT To attach a load in excess of the capacity of a circuit. In order to protect dimmers and circuits, they must always be fused to the correct capacity.

OVERLOAD CAPACITY The level of current or voltage which is the safe limit for operating a particular piece of equipment.

41

P

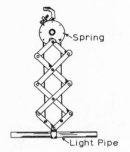

Pantograph

Par

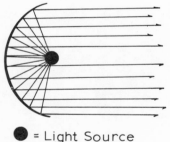

= Light Source

Parabolic Reflector

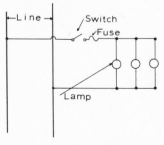

Parallel Circuit

PACKAGE DIMMER A set of dimmers which are modular.

PANEL A metal mounting plate for electrical switching systems or other electronic control systems.

PANIC SWITCH A term often referring to the switch that turns on the house lights regardless of the position of the house dimmer. This circuit should be on a different electrical source from the rest of the stage lights.

PANTOGRAPH A hanger for light instruments composed of several scissor-like parts which permit the technician to raise or lower the instrument. It is more often used in TV studios with non-lens type instruments than in theatres.

PAR Parabolic Aluminized Reflector. A heavy glass lamp which contains its own reflector and simple lens. It normally is available in flood or spot lens configurations and generally in wattages from 150 to 1,500.

PARABOLIC REFLECTOR A reflector designed to reflect light from its focal point into parallel rays. Such reflectors are found in flood lights, beam projectors, scoops, and PAR lamps.

PARALLEL CIRCUIT A battery hookup circuit in which each positive pole is fastened to one wire and each negative pole to another wire. The resulting voltage is not changed, but the amperage is equal to the sum total of each battery in the circuit. In a 120-volt, ac circuit, all lamps burn at the same intensity even if other lamps are added. No lamp is affected by the activity of the other lamps in the circuit. (See Series Circuit)

PATCH BAY (See Patch Board)

PATCH BOARD A system that permits flexibility in selecting the circuit and the particular dimmer which should function together. Such a system permits the operator to change circuits connected to the dimmer when the circuit is not in use. This frees the dimmer for another circuit and makes the system more versatile.

PATCH CORD A short electrical cord with a connector of some type on each end. It is used to make a temporary connection within circuits and is often used in patch panels of dimming systems.

PATCH PANEL (See Patch Board)

PATCH SHEET An information sheet that indicates into which dimmer a particular circuit is to be placed. It normally includes such items as the name of the play, the act, and the script page number.

PEAK LOAD The limit load which may be placed on an electrical circuit and not endanger overloading that system.

PERIOD The time of a cycle in seconds. The period of 60-cycle alternating current is 1/60 of a second.

PERSISTENT VISION The momentary continuation of the appearance of an object in the mind after the lights have been killed. This often occurs when the lights are killed rapidly.

PHANTOM LOAD (See Ghost Load)

PHASE It is the relationship of the voltage waves created by a generator in alternating current. It is possible to have a single or a three-phase system.

PHASE ANGLE The angle between the phases on a generator normally given in degrees.

PHOSPHORESCENCE The ability of some materials to absorb light energy from a light source and to continue to give off reflective light after the original source has been removed.

PHOTOMETER An instrument that measures light intensity. It is sometimes used on the stage for setting lights in order to discover hot or cold spots. It is more often used in television.

PIANO BOARD A "portable" resistance dimmer board roughly shaped like an upright piano. It is often still called a touring or road board.

PIE FORMULA (See Power Formula)

PIGTAIL An electrical terminal coming from a small piece of equipment. It is sometimes used for the cord coming from a light instrument which has the connector mounted on it.

PILE-ON To override the dimmer control with a second control. With electronic switchboards using presets, it may be necessary to increase the intensity of one or two lights. This can be accomplished by piling on. Pile-on cannot be used to decrease intensity below dimmer readings or preset.

PILOT LIGHT A small light which indicates whether or not a piece of equipment is functioning. It is usually of low voltage and wattage.

PIN CONNECTOR A fibre block with brass pins for the male plug and brass

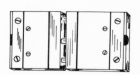

Pin Connector

43

receptacles for the female plug. It is used to connect stage cables to carry electrical current.

PIPE BATTEN A metal pipe, often about 1 inch to 2 inches outside diameter (O.D.). Light instruments are fastened to battens. The battens may be flown above the stage.

PIPE CLAMP (See "C" Clamp)

Pipe Wrench

PIPE WRENCH An adjustable wrench with steel-milled teeth on its jaws designed to hold fast to round objects such as pipe. Such a wrench is often used to join battens or to tighten light trees into their bases.

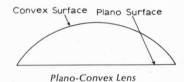

Plano-Convex Lens

PLANO-CONVEX LENS A lens which is plane (flat) on one side and convex (curve-out) on the other. The plano-convex lenx gives a sharp-edged light which is ideal for beam, booth, and balcony positions. The smaller the light source, the better the lens functions.

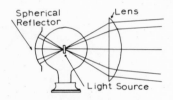

Plano-Convex Spotlight

PLANO-CONVEX SPOTLIGHTS Spotlights whose plano-convex lenses produce sharp-edged light are in this category and are therefore not limited as to location. If a diffused light is desired for blending areas on stage, frost gelatine is added to the color frame. The lights in beam, booth, or balcony position should not be frosted. The P.C. spotlights are inefficient when compared with elliposoidal and Fresnel spotlights.

PLASTICITY The ability to give three-dimensional characteristics to an object through the use of different angles of light.

PLUGGING PANEL (Patch Panel, Interconnecting Panel, Cross-Connecting Panel) A panel used for interconnecting dimmers and outlets. A plugging panel of some type is absolutely necessary if lighting equipment and switchboards are to be flexible.

PLUGS, ELECTRICAL Electrical conductors of various types designed to make temporary connections in an electrical circuit.

POCKET The metal box set flush in the stage floor or wall. It houses the receptacles into which stage cables may be plugged.

POINT SOURCE A point from which all light emenates. The closer to an actual point the light source is, the better a lens is able to function.

POLARIZED LIGHT The process by which the light energy vibrates in the same plane, direction, or straight lines.

POLE One of the terminals, positive or negative, supplying electrical energy. One end of a magnet or one electrode of a d.c. battery.

PORCELAIN A type of ceramic insulator.

PORTABLE CONTROL BOARD A light board which is readily movable from one stage to another.

POSITIVE The term used to describe the electrical pole with fewer electrons than normal which thus attracts electrons. Normally, the electrical flow is from the negative to the positive terminal. Opposite of negative.

POTENTIAL The tendency of an electric current to flow. Volts are the measure of potential.

POTENTIOMETER A small, variable resistor, similar to a radio volume control, used with electric dimmers to vary the control voltage to a dimmer and thus change the light intensity.

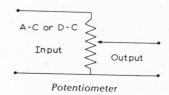

Potentiometer

POWER The rate at which energy is used. It is measured in watts.

POWER EQUATION $\dfrac{\text{Watts}}{\text{Volts}} = \text{Amps}$, or: Watts = Volts × Amps

POWER FACTOR The ratio of the voltage and current, or volt amperes, that do useful work in an alternating current circuit or equipment, to the total voltage and current, volt amperes, flowing in the electrical circuit.

POWER FORMULA This will indicate the rate of the energy used in an electrical circuit (See Ampere)

P = I × E; P = energy available, I = quantity, E = electrical pressure;
W = V × A; W = watts, V = volts, A = amperes.

POWER SWITCH The switch that connects and disconnects a particular piece of equipment from the current source. It is often called the "on-off" switch.

POWER TRANSFORMER (See Transformer)

PREFOCUS BASE A lamp base which controls the position of the filament in relationship to the reflector and the lens system.

PRESET A method of setting, in advance, light intensities on a switchboard for one or more scenes. When one scene is completed either a fader or a dimmer is used to fade lights down on that scene and up to the preset intensities of the next scene.

PRESET CONTROL (See Preset Master)

PRESET MASTER The potentiometer which controls the voltage of a complete preset bank.

Preset Control Panel

PREVENTIVE MAINTENANCE The repair or maintenance of any piece of equipment before the system fails.

PRIMARY COLORS Those colors which may be blended to make all other colors. They are red (6,150 angstroms), blue (5,200 angstroms), and green (4,470 angstroms). The blended colors cannot be blended to make the primary colors.

PRIMARY CURRENT The current which flows through the primary coil of a transformer.

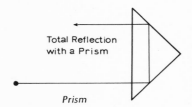

Total Reflection
with a Prism

Prism

PRIMARY WINDING The winding in the coil of a transformer which feeds the secondary coil or coils.

PRISM A transparent body with three or more sides often used to refract light.

PROGRAM To give information to the computer or memory system of a memory light board.

PROJECTION, SCENIC The technique of creating a discernible image on a screen or scenic unit through the use of lighting equipment. The image may be obtained by painted glass or plastic surfaces with a light source in back; i.e., the Linnebach projector, or by inserting a gobo in an ellipsoidal reflector.

Linnebach Projector

PUNCTURE VOLTAGE The point at which voltage, when it has been gradually increased, will penetrate the insulation.

PUSH BACK HOOKUP WIRE Stranded wire which has been tinned with solder and which has a loose insulator that may be pushed back to make connections; i.e., the asbestos wire on many theatre lighting instruments.

Q FACTOR A rating used to indicate the characteristics of coils and resonant circuits, i.e., reactance divided by ohmic resistance.

QUARTZ A hexagonal crystal which is clear and which is able to withstand a greater amount of heat than glass. For this reason, it is used in the halogen lamps.

QUARTZ-HALOGEN LAMP An incandescent lamp to which a small amount of a halogen gas (iodine, bromine) has been added. Quartz is used as the envelope because it is better able to withstand the greater heat produced by this lamp. The iodine gas tends to re-deposit the sublimated tungsten back onto the filament, thus increasing the lamp life. Because of its higher temperature, the lamp gives light in the "white" range.

QUICK-BREAK FUSE A fuse which is spring loaded. When the fuse breaks, the spring rapidly breaks the circuit and so leaves no chance for the circuit to weld together again.

RACEWAY A rectangular box, often 4" × 4", serving the same purpose as conduit. It does have a removable cover for easy access to the wires inside. Raceways often have receptacles mounted in them as are found on light battens.

RADIANT ENERGY Energy which is transmitted in the form of electromagnetic radiation is called "radiant" energy. It is generally used for light but radio waves, sound waves, and heat waves are also in this category

REACTANCE The opposition of the flow of an alternating current. Reactance is measured in ohms.

REAR PROJECTION It is an image projected on the rear of a translucent screen. Its advantage is that the actors will not project their shadows on the screen. It requires a screen with a high dispersion rate so that the hot spot of the light instrument will not be visible to the audience.

RECEPTACLE A permanent electrical installation to which equipment can be attached. The load, or equipment, is plugged into the receptacle.

RECTIFIER A device which changes the pattern of alternating current to direct current.

REFLECTANCE The capability of a surface to reflect light, measured as the ratio of the incidental light to the reflected light from the given surface. It is normally expressed in per cent.

REFLECTANCE A measurement of the efficiency of a given surface to reflect light or any other wave pattern.

REFLECTION (See Angle of Reflection)

REFLECTION The condition when a wave, i.e., light, strikes a different medium and is then returned to the original medium. (See Angle of Incidence)

Receptacle

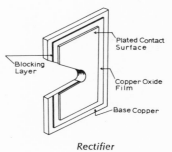

Rectifier

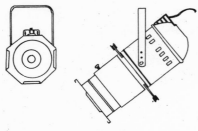

Ellipsoidal Reflector

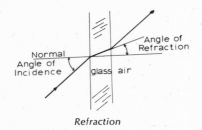

Refraction

REFLECTION LAW The angle of incidence is equal to the angle of reflection (See Angle of Reflection)

REFLECTORS Reflectors are usually highly polished metal or mirror, concave in shape, used with spotlights. Floodlights and border lights, however, generally have reflectors of a dull metal. Efficiency of reflectors ranges from about 10 per cent for light-colored surfaces to about 90 per cent for mirrored glass or alzak reflectors. Reflectors may be Spherical, Ellipsoidal, or Parabolic.

REFRACTION This is the "bending" of light rays when they pass from one medium to another. A lens refracts light to concentrate it on a given point called the focal point. Focal lengths are expressed in inches from the lens center to the point where rays of light converge.

REGULATOR, VOLTAGE A device which is so designed that it is able to maintain a set voltage.

RELAY An electro-mechanical device which opens or closes contacts through the use of a coil and armature.

RELAY An electromagnetic device which actuates an electrical circuit by magnetically opening or closing a given set of contact points.

RELIABILITY The capability of a particular piece of equipment to function under prescribed conditions and for a prescribed period of time.

REMOTE CONTROL A system by which the control of any piece of equipment is preformed from a distance through some signal, often electrical, conveyed through wires.

REMOTE ERROR SENSING The method by which a regulator circuit tests the output voltage of a dimmer and makes voltage adjustments to compensate for any errors.

RESISTANCE The friction or resistance to the passage of electricity offered by any conductor. The amount of resistance is affected by material, diameter, length, and temperature. Resistance is expressed in ohms.

RESISTANCE DIMMER A dimmer which adds enough resistance to the current flow so that the lamp will no longer light. Four times the resistance of the lamp is required for the dimmer to produce the blackout. Heat is created by this process.

RESISTOR A device which resists the flow of electric current in a wire.

RETRIEVE To recall information from a memory light board system.

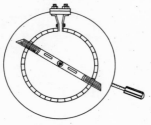

Resistance Dimmer

REVERSIBLE MOTOR A motor which is equipped with a switch that changes the polarity of the current and thus makes the motor go in an opposite direction.

REVERSING SWITCH A switch that changes the polarity of a circuit so as to change the rotation of an electric motor.

R.F.I (Radio frequency interference) It is the energy caused by ac power which can interfere with electronic audio signals. Most power dimming equipment incorporates R.F.I. filters.

RHEOSTAT A variable resistor which regulates the current in a circuit by varying the resistance in series with the load.

RIGID CONDUIT Metal conduit which is thick enough for the cutting of standard thread. This makes it possible for the pipe to be joined with threaded couplings instead of with sleeves and set screws as is done in thin wall conduit.

RISER The ridge left inside a stepped lens or on the outside of a Fresnel lens when the glass has been removed is called a "riser." A stepped lens often has blackened risers to control stray light.

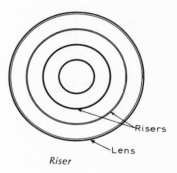

Riser

ROAD BOARD (See Piano Board)

ROMEX CONNECTOR A threaded metal connector used to tie electrical wires to a metal outlet box.

ROSIN A material which aids in joining metals when they are being soldered.

ROSIN-CORE SOLDER Solder which has rosin flux in its center.

ROTARY GENERATOR (See Generator, AC)

ROUND BEAM A term often used in opposition to the oval beam produced by a Fresnel light instrument with a special oval beam lens.

ROUNDEL (Rondel) A round or concave, heat-resistant, glass, color filter available for certain types of border lights and footlights. Color selection in roundels is greatly limited in comparison with gelatine, but the colors will not fade.

RUPTURE The tearing apart or bursting, as of the insulation around an electrical wire.

S

SATURATION A term used to describe a color which has no addition of white, black, or other colors.

"S" Cable

"S" CABLE An electrical cable with a heavy rubber shield. At the present time, it is illegal for use under OSHA regulations.

SCENE MASTER A potentiometer that controls a given group of dimmers which have been switched into a particular scene setting.

SCIOPTICON A motorized attachment to a spot light, often an ellipsoidal reflector, which includes a condensing lens and a rotating pattern. It is generally used to create the effect of moving clouds, snow, or rain.

Scoop Light

SCOOPS These are spun-aluminum parobolic reflectors with no outside housings. They are light in weight and are particularly adaptable as hanging floodlights or for lighting cycloramas. Scoops are designed for 300- to 500-watt or 750- to 2,000-watt lamps. They offer greater concentration of light than old-style standard floods.

SCR (See Silicon Controlled Rectifier)

SCREW BASE The type of base for a lamp which is inserted by turning it. When it is tight, the electrical connection is made. This type of base is used for floodlights, border lights, and strip lights.

SEALED BEAM LIGHTS (PAR) A type of light which has a parabolic aluminized reflector built into the bulb or lamp, thus directionalizing the beam of light and increasing its efficiency. The most frequently used types are 150-watt spotlights or footlights.

SEC An abbreviation for the second or the secondary winding of a transformer.

SECONDARY This is the winding of the output phase of a transformer. The voltage is adjusted because of the relationship of the primary coil and the secondary coil.

SECONDARY COLORS These are the colors created through the mixing of equal amounts of the primary colors. The secondary colors are yellow (5,780 angstroms), magenta and purple (4,020 angstroms), and blue-green (5,080 angstroms).

SECONDARY VOLTAGE This generally refers to the voltage which comes from the secondary windings of a transformer.

SECONDARY WINDING It is the winding of the secondary coil in a transformer.

SELECTIVE ABSORPTION The ability of a painted surface to absorb certain colors or light waves. If all the light waves are absorbed then the surface will appear black.

SELECTIVE REFLECTANCE The ability of a painted surface to reflect certain colors or light waves. If all light waves are present (white light), and the surface reflects all these waves, then the surface will appear white.

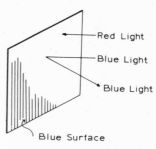

Selective Reflectance

SELF RESET Any interrupting device which returns to its normal state, often used with circuit breakers.

SERIES A method of connecting electrical components in such a way that they lower the voltage of the circuit by direct ratio to the division of the number of components on that circuit.

SERIES CIRCUIT Any equipment that is wired to form a conductor; e.g, a series of lamp sockets with alternate binding posts connected so that the current must flow through each lamp in order to complete the circuit. The path of electricity passes through each lamp filament before continuing to the next, resulting in a voltage loss in direct relation to the number of lamps in the circuit. Thus, in a 110-volt circuit wired in series with ten lamps of equal intensity, the voltage for each lamp would be eleven, and intensity would be lessened accordingly. Batteries wired in series increase total voltage to the sum of the voltage of each battery. Usually switches, most dimmers, and fuses are placed in series.

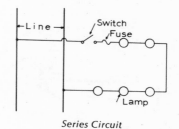

Series Circuit

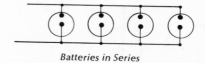

Batteries in Series

SERIES CONNECTION The method of connecting resistances end to end in order to make a complete series circuit.

SERIES MOTOR An electrical motor in which the field and the armature have been connected in series.

SERIES RESISTOR A resistor which is placed in series in an electrical circuit. It is often used to adjust the voltage to a particular requirement of a piece of equipment.

SERVICE DROP The electrical conductors between the last line power pole and the first point of attachment to the building.

SERVICE ENTRANCE EQUIPMENT This said of electrical power which comes into the building before it is fused and distributed to the rest of the building. Often high voltage is found in this area where only highly qualified personnel should proceed with caution.

SERVO MOTOR An electrical motor whose rotating speed is controlled by corrective electrical impulses.

SET LIGHTS To focus the lighting equipment for a play.

SHADE A result caused by the addition of black to a color. It is a term more often used in relation to pigment.

SHELF LIFE The period of time that batteries (or any other material) can remain out of use and still be usable.

SHIELDING The practice of controlling the magnetic field created by an electric cable by surrounding it with a grounded shield. It is a practice often used with electronic sound cables.

SHORT CIRCUIT A uncontrolled flow of electricity which results in a blown fuse.

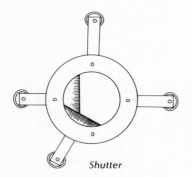

Shutter

SHUTTER A metal gate, usually in sets of four, placed at the aperture of an ellipsoidal reflector. Shutters enable the operator to change the shape of the light beam.

Side Arm Pipe Clamp

SIDE ARM PIPE CLAMP A "C" clamp with a short pipe attached to it, often used for mounting spot lights in tormentor positions. It is also used to clamp to a batten with the pipe in an upward position next to a line; the line is then tied to this short pipe, thus preventing the batten from twisting if light instruments are hung on it.

SILICON CONTROLLED RECTIFIERS: (SCR's) These are transitor-like devices which control the current by providing "gates" to control the flow of electricity. They are light and compact in size and are highly efficient.

SINE WAVE A wave which may be stated as the sine of the linear function of space and time.

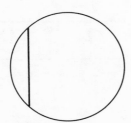

Single Phase Winding Symbol

SINGLE PHASE An electrical system with two hot wires and one common or neutral wire. Either 120-volt or 220-volt single phase may be obtained.

SINGLE POLE, DOUBLE THROW A switch with three terminals which may connect one terminal to either of the other two. Such switches are often found in light consoles to connect potentiometers to master circuits or preset systems.

Single Pole, Double Throw

SINGLE POLE SWITCH A switch that breaks only one side of the wiring system. The common wire should be left intact and the hot wire broken by the switch.

SIX BY NINE (See Lens Sizes)

SKIN BACK To peel off the insulator from a wire before fastening the end to a connector.

SKY CYC (See Cyclorama)

SKY PAN A shallow scoop which gives off light at a very wide angle. It is often used for the lighting of a cyclorama or other backdrop.

SLIDE A movable contact which changes position by sliding in a forward or backward motion rather than by turning. Areal Davis dimmers often use such a device.

SLIDE SWITCH A switch that moves from one contact to another by sliding to and fro rather than by functioning on a rocker. Slide switches often have several contacts to which they may be moved.

SLIP RING A device used for making electrical connections from a stationary to a rotating object.

SNAKE A thin, metal tape or wire which is pushed through a conduit run so that electrical cable can be attached to it and pulled through.

SNAP SWITCH A switch that makes the actual contact because of the movement of a spring. The initial movement is made manually by the operator.

SNOOT (See Funnel)

"SO" CABLE An electrical cable with a heavy rubber shield which is oil resistant, as required by OSHA regulations.

SOCKET A support into which the base of a lamp can be placed so that an electrical contact is made.

SOCKET ADAPTOR A device which changes the configuration of the support socket so that a different type of base may be inserted into it.

SOFT LIGHT A term for light which is spread evenly over a surface.

SOLDER A soft metal which is melted around electrical wires when they are twisted together. This forms a solid connection.

SOLENOID A movable iron core which is mounted inside a coil. It is moved when current activates the magnet and moves the iron core which, in turn, may be connected to the work load.

SOLID GROUND A ground which shows no impedance and which normally is not fused.

SOLID NEUTRAL The neutral in a three- or four-wire system which is not fused or broken in any way.

SOLID STATE A general term used for equipment which functions through the use of semiconductors rather than vacuum tubes.

SOURCE That part of the electrical system which provides the electrical energy.

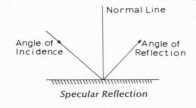

Spectrum

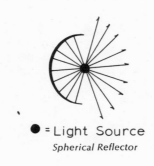

Specular Reflection

SPARK A brilliant flash caused by a momentarily uncontrolled flow between two electrodes.

SPECIFIC ILLUMINTATION (Key Lighting) A highly directional light. It tends to give shadows which denote the shape and direction of the lights. It is the opposite of general illumination.

SPECTRAL HUES The colors which the human eye recognizes. They consist of a single wavelength or, at most, a very narrow band of wavelengths.

SPECTROANALYSIS The technique of measuring the amount of each wavelength which is present in a given beam of light. This will specify the color or colors present in that beam of light.

SPECTRUM The continum of electromagnetic radiations ranging from the long radio waves to the short cosmic rays. Light radiations fall within this group: Blue having the shorter wave length of about 4,000 angstroms and Red having the longer wave length of about 7,000 angstroms.

SPECULAR REFLECTION The reflection given off by a mirror-like surface which reflects light beams at the same angle of reflection as the angle of incidence. The light tends to remain in one "beam" rather than being spread.

SPHERICAL ABERRATION The failure of a lens or reflector to focus all rays of light from a source to a given point. This causes stray beams of light to spill in a most objectionable manner. (See Light Spill)

SPHERICAL REFLECTOR A reflector which is a section of a circle. It requires that the light point source be at the center. It is often used in Fresnel light instruments.

● = Light Source

Spherical Reflector

Western Union

Splice

SPILL A term given to stray beams of light or uncontrolled light which strikes the stage or any other area where it is not wanted. Spill is sometimes caused by imperfect lenses which should be replaced, or by dusty lenses which should be cleaned. (See Light Spill)

SPILL RINGS (Louvers) These consist of a series of concentric metal rings or parallel slats used to direct a beam of light and to control spill.

SPLICE A coupling between two wires which possesses both mechanical strength and conductivity.

SPLICING The act of joining electrical wires together so that the joint is electrically and mechanically sound. Normal splices used are Western Union splice, Tap splice, and Pigtail splice.

SPOT An abbreviation for a spotlight.

SPOTLIGHTS (Spot) These are lights equipped with a lens and, in most types, a sliding lamp socket and reflector for adjusting the focus. There are several types of spots: Baby spots, 100-, 250-, 400-watts; Plano-convex 500-2,000-watts; Ellipsoidal 500-, 3,000-watts; Fresnel 500-3,000-watts; Arc lights 2,500-10,000-watts.

SPREAD OF SPOTLIGHT This is the area covered by the light from a spotlight. It is determined by the size, focal length of lens, and distance from the light source to the stage floor.

SPREAD REFLECTION The reflection given off by a surface which causes most of the light beam to reflect at the angle of reflection.

SQUARE LAW CURVE In dimming equipment it is the curve which adjusts the level of light intensity exactly to that of the dimmer setting. Thus, if the setting is changed from 50% to 60%, the light intensity will increase by only 10%. This curve is often used with the newer electronic dimmers. (See Linear Curve)

STAGE LEFT The left side of the stage when facing the audience. The term is often used to indicate the movement toward that side. (See Stage Right)

STAGE PLUG A dated plug originally designed for the high amperage in non-flexible theatres. It consists of a center brace of some non-conductive material with brass plates, or bus bars, in floor pockets. Stage plugs are not safe and do not comply with present safety codes because there is a definite possibility of the operator's coming in contact with live wires when connecting the stage plug.

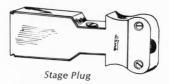

Stage Plug

STAGE RIGHT The right side of the stage when facing the audience. The term is often used to indicate the movement toward that side. (See Stage Left)

STANDARD (See Light Tree)

STEP-DOWN TRANSFORMER It is a transformer which reduces the line voltage to a given point. (See Transformer)

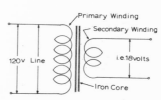

Step-Down Transformer

STEP-LENS (Stepped Lens) This is a lens which is the reverse of the Fresnel lens. The step-lens has risers on the plane (flat) side of the lens, leaving the convex side in its original curve. The step-lens is lightweight, heat resistant, and it produces a hard-edged light suitable for beam. However, a sharper focus can be obtained with a double plano-convex lens system.

STEP-UP TRANSFORMER It is a transformer which increases the voltage because of the ratio of the windings of the primary and secondary coils.

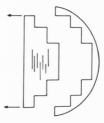

Step-Lens

STILSON WRENCH (See Pipe Wrench)

STORAGE ACCESS TIME The time it takes for the information given to a computer or memory system to accept the information, store it, and make it available for recall.

STRAND The name given any single piece of wire from stranded wire. (See Stranded Wire)

STRANDED WIRE A wire composed of a number of fine wires twisted or bunched together, thus making the cable more flexible.

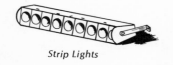

Strip Lights

STRIP LIGHTS These are lights which are similar to border lights, with three color circuits, and designed for roundel glass filters or colored R-40 or PAR-38 lamps. They are now most commonly used between groundrows on the floor below eye level. They may also be used for horizon or cyclorama lighting.

STRIP OUT A term meaning to cover the stage with a wide beam of light from a follow spot, as opposed to the general practice of following the actor with a narrow cone of light.

STROBE LIGHT A high-intensity lamp designed to flash at variable rates. It contains a gas-filled tube which fires when a high voltage source, such as a capacitor, is activated.

Strobe Light

SUBLIMATION Said of the changing of a metal (the filament) to a gas without going through a melting period.

SUN SPOT (See Beam Projector)

SWITCHBOARDS These are control boards consisting of the fuses, switches, and dimmers necessary to control stage lights. Switchboards ideally have sufficient dimmers to control the lights for each area of the stage, plus special effects lights, general toning lights, cyclorama lights, and house lights. There are several types of switchboards: piano, preset, and remote control.

SWITCHES Devices for making and breaking electrical circuits. There are several types of switches: circuit breaker (breaker switch), knife, master, mercury, rotary, selector, and toggle.

T

TAP A permanent connectable location on an electrical piece of equipment; e.g., a 6-, 8-, or 12-volt transforꞏner will have permanent taps at those voltages.

TEMPLATE A term sometimes used for the metal inserts used in Ellipsoidal light instruments to project simple patterns. (For a more common usage, see Cookie)

TERMINAL One end of an electrical circuit, usually providing a means of attaching a conductor.

TERMINAL BOARD An insulated base with some attaching device such as set screws, so that conductors can be connected to it easily.

TERMINAL PROTECTOR A device which is heat sensitive and is able to disconnect any piece of equipment which overheats.

THERMAL CIRCUIT BREAKER A circuit breaker which is actuated when the temperature caused by the current flow is sufficient to cause a metalic strip to bend, thus causing the contact points to open.

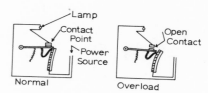
Thermal Circuit Breaker

THIN WALL CONDUIT Metal conduit which is too thin for threads to be cut into it as can be done in rigid wall conduit. Sleeves with set screws are used to join thin wall conduit. (See Rigid Conduit)

THREE PHASE An electrical system which has three hot wires and one common wire.

Three Phase

THREE WIRE SYSTEM A single phase system which uses two hot wires and one common wire. Since it is a single phase system, the two hot legs use the same common or neutral wire for the return. This is possible because the sine waves of the two hot legs fluctuate in opposite manner.

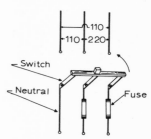
Three Wire Power System

THROW The distance between lighting instruments and the area to be illuminated. A practical throw of a given instrument is the distance between the instrument and an intensity reading of 35 foot-candles on a photometer.

TINNED WIRE Wire which has been dipped in solder. This is often done so that multiple-strand wire will become solidified at the tips for better fastening to a connector.

TINT The result caused by the addition of white to a color. It is a term more often used in relation to pigment.

TOGGLE SWITCH A small switch which uses a spring-loaded straight lever to connect or disconnect a circuit.

Toggle Switch Assembly

TOLERANCE The permissable variation away from the rated levels.

TONING LIGHTS A term that sometimes refers to those lights used for general color and mood.

Transformer

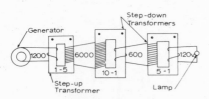

Transformers in Action

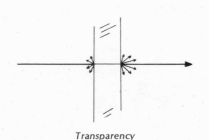

Transparency

TOP HAT (See Funnel)

TOP LIGHTING A method of lighting in which light is brought down on the actor so as to give more dimension to the body. It tends to create a slight halo around the head of the actor and thus forces attention to the head.

TORMENTOR BATTEN A vertical pipe used for the mounting of the tormentor light instruments. This pipe is usually positioned as far down stage as possible.

TORMENTOR LIGHT A light mounted on a tower in back of the tormentor. The tormentor is usually mounted just upstage of the proscenium arch.

TORM LIGHT (See Tormentor Light)

TOWER A term which is used interchangeably with "Light Tree." It is a rectangular structure usually made of metal, possibly as simple as one pipe, to which light instruments may be fastened.

TRANSFORMER A core of laminated iron on which two coils of wire are wound. A primary coil, carrying alternating current, induces an alternating current in the secondary coil. Voltage in the secondary coil is determined by the ratio of windings on the primary coil to the windings on the secondary coil. The more windings on the secondary, the higher the voltage.

TRANSISTOR A semiconductor device usually made of silicon.

TRANSLUCENT Said of a material which permits light to penetrate, but which tends to diffuse the light.

TRANSMISSION LINE A material (usually metalic) which forms a continuous path from one location to another. The transmission line forms a path for electromagnetic energy so that it may be conducted from one place to another.

TRANSMITTANCE A measurement of the relative efficiency of a given material to transmit light; i.e., the ratio of transmitted lumens to the incident lumens on the material.

TRANSPARENT Said of a material which permits light to penetrate, but which does not diffuse the light.

TREE (See Light Tree)

TRIAC The trade name of General Electric for a dimming device much like an SCR. It is a gating-controlled device which can be switched from a blocking to a conducting state, thus requiring only one per dimmer. It produces less "hum" than the SCR dimmer.

TRICKLE CHARGE A very slow charge on a battery, about equal to the loss rate of the battery in storage.

TRIPLEX CABLE A cable composed of three individually insulated wires bound together by a common cover or insulator.

TUNGSTEN A metal with a high melting point, often used in incandescent lamps and on the surface of electrical contact points in switches.

TUNGSTEN-HALOGEN (See Quartz-Halogen Lamp)

TWIN CABLE A cable composed of two individually insulated wires bound together by a common cover or insulator.

TWIST-LOCK CONNECTOR A connector having prongs made with hooks to prevent the connector from coming apart without first being untwisted.

TWOFER Said of two female (line) receptacles tied to a single male (load) plug. (See Multiple)

TWO PHASE An alternating current circuit in which there are two currents in phases which are 90 degrees opposed. More often, it is called single phase.

TWO-WIRE SYSTEM An electrical system consisting of one hot wire and one common wire but no ground wire. In the United States where such a system is found, it is generally a 120-volt system. Presently this system is only found in some of the older theatres and with some occasional touring groups.

Two Phase

U

U-BOLT A metal bolt threaded at both ends, shaped like a "U," and having a plate on the open end which may be tightened down with nuts. U-bolts are often used as cable clamps on light battens.

"UL" LABEL A label which indicates that the equipment which carries it has been tested and meets the minimum standards of the Underwriters Laboratories, Inc., 207 E. Ohio Street, Chicago, Illinois 60611.

ULTRAVIOLET The color which is below, or has a longer wavelength than, the visible violet which is about 4,000 angstroms. (See Black Light)

UNBALANCED Said of a condition which results when the legs of the incoming power have different loads on them.

UNDER LIGHTING Low intensity lighting used to establish a desired mood. The light intensity, however, should not be so low as to strain the viewer's eyes.

UNGROUNDED A circuit which is not connected to a ground.

UNIT A term sometimes used to indicate a light instrument or a luminaire.

UPSTAGE The area of the stage furthest from the audience. The term is also used to indicate the movement away from the audience from any area of the stage. (See Downstage)

V

VARIABLE RESISTOR A term sometimes used for a potentiometer or a rheostat.

VARIABLE TRANSFORMER A transformer in which the windings on the secondary coil are exposed so that any voltage may be tapped from the transformer.

VARIABLE VOLTAGE TRANSFORMER (See Autotransformer)

VELOCITY OF LIGHT 186,283 statute miles per second.

VISIBLE SPECTRUM The wavelengths of light which can be seen by the human eye. They range from 3,800 angstroms (blue-violet) to 7,600 angstroms (deep red).

VOLT An electromotive force, or difference of electrical potential, which will cause a current of one amp to flow through a conductor against a resistance of one ohm. Most stage circuits in the United States carry a potential of 110-120 volts.

VOLTAGE DROP The lowering or loss of voltage because of the current's flowing through an impedance. Small wire size, if used over extended distances, will lead to voltage drops.

VOLTAGE TRANSFORMER (See Transformer)

V.O.M. Volt Ohm Meter. A device which is able to measure a wide range of ac/dc voltages and ohms.

WALL OUTLET A permanently installed receptacle.

WARM COLORS A general reference to those colors ranging from 5,500 to 7,000 angstroms. These would include the reds and yellows which are often used in combinations.

WASH LIGHTS Light instruments used in wide focus for general coverage to provide fill light. This type of lighting is contrasted with sharply focused instruments used to highlight or illuminate a specific area.

WATT The unit of measured of electric power. Watts = Amps x Volts Lighting instruments are rated in watts.

WATTAGE RATING The maximum power a piece of equipment may safely carry.

WHITE The term used to refer to the condition resulting when a surface is able to reflect all the wavelengths in the visible spectrum.

WIRE A stranded or solid metal conductor. In electrical terms, it is generally covered with an insulator. Dimensions of wire are indicated by gauge number. (See Gauge)

WIRE NUT A plastic cap which is twisted over two or more wires that are to be joined. This is an improvement over the use of electrical tape because the plastic is more resistant to heat and abrasion.

WIREWAY (See Raceway)

WORK LIGHTS Permanently installed light instruments which provide sufficient light for the general work occurring on the stage; i.e., rehearsals, setting up, or the construction of scenery. Usually work lights are not on a dimmed circuit.

WYE CONNECTION This connection produces a three-phase or four-wire electrical system. Each leg A, B, C, produces 120 volts when connected to ground. When the hot legs are shared, they produce 208 volts. The advantage of a Wye connection over a Delta connection is that each of the legs may be used. Often, Wye connection is written as "Y" connection.

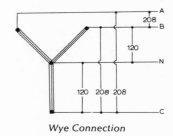

Wye Connection

XENON LAMP An arc lamp mounted in a glass envelope in the presence of xenon gas. The lamp gives an intense light of very high color temperature (6,000 degrees Kelvin). It has a very small light source when compared to an incandescent lamp and uses very little power. It operates on dc voltages and thus requires an ac converter. Since the envelope is under high pressure, these lamps are dangerous. Xenon lamps cannot be dimmed.

Y CONNECTION (See Wye Connection)

YOKE The "U"-shaped brace which is used to support the light instrument at the open end. It is drilled at the other end to accept a "C" clamp for mounting the instrument to a batten or other pipe.